ava
academia

An AVA Book

Published by AVA Publishing SA
Rue des Fontenailles 16
Case Postale
1000 Lausanne 6
Switzerland
Tel: +41 786 005 109
Email: enquiries@avabooks.ch

Distributed by Thames & Hudson
(ex-North America)
181a High Holborn
London WC1V 7QX
United Kingdom
Tel: +44 20 7845 5000
Fax: +44 20 7845 5055
Email: sales@thameshudson.co.uk
www.thamesandhudson.com

Distributed in the USA & Canada by:
Ingram Publisher Services Inc.
1 Ingram Blvd.
La Vergne TN 37086
USA
Tel: +1 866 400 5351
Fax: +1 800 838 1149
Email: customer.service@
ingrampublisherservices.com

English Language Support Office
AVA Publishing (UK) Ltd.
Tel: +44 1903 204 455
Email: enquiries@avabooks.ch

Copyright © AVA Publishing SA 2010

The author asserts her moral rights to the work.
Email: kathryn.best@btopenworld.com

ISBN 978-2-940411-07-8

10 9 8 7 6 5 4 3 2 1

Design by:
Anne Odling-Smee
John F McGill

Production by:
AVA Book Production Pte. Ltd, Singapore
Tel: +65 6334 8173
Fax: +65 6259 9830
Email: production@avabooks.com.sg

All reasonable attempts have been made to
trace, clear and credit the copyright holders
of the images reproduced in this book. However,
if any credits have been inadvertently omitted,
the publisher will endeavour to incorporate
amendments in future editions.

Kathryn Best

The Fundamentals
of Design
Management

Ethical:
aware-
ness/
reflect-
ion/
debate

ava
academia

1

2

3

4

5

6

How to get the most out of this book

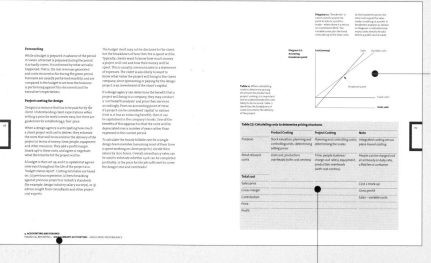

Section headings
Provide a brief outline of the key concepts and ideas that the chapter will explore.

Captions
Supply contextual information about the images and help connect the visuals with those key concepts discussed in the body copy.

Diagrams
Help to explain design management theory and its application in more detail.

Navigation
Chapter navigation helps you determine which chapter unit you are in and what the preceding and following sections are.

Tables and box outs
Contain more detailed and contextual information about practices and concepts that are referred to in the body copy.

Case studies
Explore the ideas discussed within each chapter through a practical examination of real-life applications.

Colour coding
Enables easy navigation of chapters.

Contextual perspectives
Interviews with industry professionals highlight key themes.

The Fundamentals of Design Management is intended to provide you with a general overview of design management in an easily digestible, but informative and interesting way. It is based on the insight and practice of design managers working professionally within the industry. Interviews with key figures employed in different sectors of the creative industries tease out their knowledge of design management and provide perspectives on their working practices through real-life examples.

Case studies also feature at the end of Chapters 2–6 and provide an opportunity for you to explore the ideas, skills and knowledge that you have learnt from the content within each chapter. This book will provide you with a solid foundation in the study of design management; and will also appeal to people already working in business who are keen to obtain practical knowledge and theoretical insights about the discipline of design management.

Introduction

8

Design management is about the successful management of the people, projects, processes and procedures behind the design of our everyday products, services, environments and experiences.

Equally, design management is about the management of the relationships between different disciplines (such as design, management, marketing and finance) and different roles (such as clients, designers, project teams and stakeholders).

The creative industries (also known as the creative economy) include the areas of design, arts and crafts, advertising, architecture, fashion, film, music, TV, radio, performing arts, publishing and interactive software. Current global trends related to creativity in design businesses identify the creative industries as one of the fastest-growing sectors in the world and one of the best ways to increase competitive advantage between commercial companies and even entire countries. In addition, there is growing demand for taking a more holistic approach to the cultural, environmental, political and societal impact of how commercial businesses and other organisations operate. And because design, by its very nature, takes a people-centred approach to problem-solving, it is well positioned to enable a more integrative, holistic approach to solving contemporary 'world' challenges.

Design does not operate in isolation from other disciplines and professions, but in relation to a wide range of different conditions. The external context around design is evident in business, society, technology, politics and the environment. It is also evident in design's relationship to the worlds of marketing, management, engineering, finance, law and economics. The internal context around design includes how branding and innovation, user and market research, client briefs and design audits, budgets and teams, and project aims and objectives, can be leveraged to harness the power of design activity for the benefit of business, society and the economy.

Managing how design can have a positive impact and how it can operate holistically in relation to all these internal and external contexts, disciplines and roles, relationships and connections, is one of the main challenges faced by anyone learning about and working within design, business and the creative industries today.

Design is present in tangible form – in the people, the projects and the products and services with which we come into contact every day. These are referred to as the 'touchpoints' of design, and form an important part of how designers and managers consider, for example, the way people experience an organisation or a brand.

But design is also present intangibly in the working processes and inter-disciplinary relationships that are part of the integrative nature of design practice:

• how we manage the relationships between people – the clients, the design consultancies, the stakeholders and end-users or customers.

• how we organise the teams, the processes and procedures of any design project.

• deciding how products and services come to market – the linking of the systems, the places and the final delivery of a designed and managed customer experience.

Bringing any product, service or experience to market often requires extensive input and support from a wide range of different people, with different areas of expertise, capabilities and skills. And the way in which the people, processes and projects are managed can have an enormous impact on the success, or failure, of the final outcome. The study of design management concerns itself with how to bring all these people, projects and processes together, in an inter-disciplinary and collaborative framework within a wider business, societal, political and environmental context, and in a way that takes into account a multitude of considerations to form a coherent, financially viable and delightfully crafted experience.

One of the most valuable aspects of design management as an approach is that it provides a framework for new processes to be implicitly integrated into existing approaches and methodologies. Design is a problem-solving process where an actual design 'problem' is also a design 'opportunity'; to consider, if necessary, a new approach or engage different stakeholders in finding a solution, if the process of problem-solving identifies this as a need. For example, currently there are increased trends in the areas of co-design, inclusive/universal design (where the needs of a wider range of people are taken into account) and sustainability (where the long-term impact is considered).

In addition, designers are increasingly expected to work alongside other specialists (for example, marketers, engineers, social scientists), necessitating an understanding of the wider context in which design operates (for example, commercial business or societal challenges). Their contributions to a given project may be made as an individual, as part of a multidisciplinary team or as part of a larger collaborative or collective working process enabled by new technologies.

Design in context

Design and business cultures

Design and business have their own distinct cultures: their own beliefs, values and assumptions about how they measure success and what matters to them. This can sometimes create a 'clash of cultures'. To be more influential in the creative industries, a better understanding of the challenges and opportunities inherent in different organisational cultures is a powerful advantage.

The creative industries are fundamentally interconnected. Designers need to be aware of standard business and management processes and practices, and the dependent ways in which different enterprises relate and operate. Equally, business needs an appreciation of discipline-specific and inter-disciplinary design processes and practices, and their potential for enabling change.

Currently, many business cultures do not understand the value of, or investment of time and money in, the design process. And many design professionals do not know how to justify the value of design. In effect, 'clients don't know how to buy design, and creatives don't know how to sell it' (Loglisci, 2009). Undervaluing the process of design, by both parties, devalues the profession of design. Taking a responsible approach to making clear the difference between design and business practices is a start.

Design

Design is a people-centred, problem-solving process. To design (verb) is to plan, to create or to devise. It is a process, a practice and a way of thinking. A design (noun) has form and function; it is the outcome of the process of designing. Design professionals operate within businesses either on the client side (as in-house designers within established business functions and departments), or on the agency/consultancy side (within inter-disciplinary client/project teams or single-discipline clusters). Designers also operate in a freelance capacity, bringing expertise to projects both inside and outside organisations. The role of design is expanding in scope to encompass more areas, using its people-centred approach to cross traditional functional boundaries, both client and agency-side.

Examples of design disciplines: Graphic design, packaging design, product design, industrial design, interior/environmental design, digital media/web design, service design, experience design.

Typical design consultancy functions: Creative/design, client account direction and management, business/strategic consultancy, project management, finance, administration, PR/marketing.

Client-side functions in which design is typically present: Design, new product/service development, brand communications, marketing communications, research and development, technology/IT.

Management

The term 'management' refers to the people and processes involved in managing, organising, controlling and administering a business. Frequently, the world of business and management, focused on financial rewards and profit-making incentives, is at odds with the people-centred, problem-solving process of design. The advantages of design may be lost if not sheltered from traditional management controls and incentives; equally, design needs the protection and restraints of an efficient, effective management framework.

Business

A business is a legally recognised commercial enterprise set up to provide goods and services to consumers or organisations. It is a profit-seeking entity intended to generate a financial return in exchange for work done, time spent and risks taken. Viable businesses satisfy a market need and make a profit; those that don't fall into debt and often close.

The most common business structures are:

Sole trader (sole proprietor): a business owned by one person who is solely liable for the business and any profits made or debts incurred. They may employ and work with other individuals.

Partnership: a business owned by two or more people who divide equally all profits and losses. They share full, personal and unlimited liability for the partnership and any debts incurred. Partnerships can be general, unlimited, or limited liability.

Limited liability company (Private or Public): acts in a similar way to partnerships, but the owners have no personal liability.

Corporation: a business that is legally separate from its owners (the owners are in fact the shareholders, who have limited liability). It is overseen by a board of directors, which hires managerial staff to run the corporation. Assets and liabilities belong to the corporation, not the owners.

Cooperative: has members (instead of shareholders) who share decision-making authority.

Examples of business sectors: Retail, real estate, transportation, utilities, manufacturing, finance, agriculture, professional service industries or creative industries.

Examples of business functions: Human resources, finance, sales and marketing, PR/communications, IT, operations, procurement, research and development.

Design and management temperaments: Individuals, and whole professions, tend to think in particular ways; understanding these different approaches (below) is an important part of being a design manager.

Right brain – analytical, structured, linear, compartmentalising, decisive, controlled.

Left brain – holistic, unstructured, iterative, assimilative, questioning, intuitive.

Finance, technology and law

Leveraging the impact of design requires awareness of areas currently undergoing change – areas such as technology, finance and law – and adopting new processes as a consequence. Technology is enabling closer relationships between users (and how they participate) and content (and how it is developed). The phrase 'Web 2.0' describes a range of technology-enabled design approaches such as open-source software and user-generated content, evidenced in offers such as Ebay, YouTube and Wikipedia. These approaches are also changing how we relate to, manage and interact with our legal and financial systems, and how these systems are responding with, for example, new forms of Intellectual Property (IP) protection and digital rights, and new ways to think about the concept and meaning of financial capital. A starting point to how we think about design in relation to these systems is to look at the concepts of finance, technology and law.

Finance

Finance deals with the management of money, that is, supplying or raising money, and managing the relationship between money, time and risk.

The most universally accepted form of money today is cash – banknotes, coins and current account deposits – but, in effect, money could be anything that is readily accepted as a form of payment or exchange of value.

The financial intermediaries who provide credit (*loans*) to facilitate funding (*cash*) are called banks. Banks mediate between lenders (*who charge interest*) and borrowers (*who pay interest*). Banks and other similar financial service providers manage the financial assets and the associated risks inherent in trading assets (*investments*), equity (*stocks and shares*), debts/securities (*bonds*) and insurance (*against loss*), on security exchanges (*trading facilities for stockbrokers*) throughout the world.

In the financial services industry, money is 'a token of wealth' (Boyle, 2003), exchanged in the form of abstract numbers – whether currency, shares, stocks and bonds. These digital flows of intangible money and capital form the financial system. According to Boyle, money started as a form of ritual gift – as a way to make peace; it was about mutual recognition and facilitating human relationships and, only later, became a means of trading. Our current financial system, however, has replaced human relationships with monetary ones.

1. The Co-operative Bank, based in the United Kingdom, has a unique customer-led Ethical Policy which means it will not invest in businesses that operate in areas of concern to their customers. The Co-operative Investments and The Co-operative Insurance take a different approach, listening to customer views expressed in their Ethical Engagement Policies; using their influence as a corporate shareholder to seek to change big companies from the inside.

1

The **co-operative** bank
good with money

Currently, there is a need for a fairer form of capitalism and a financial system that thinks long term. Short-term decision-making – even if profitable for share traders and shareholders – often has long-term consequences that can ultimately harm communities and other stakeholders.

Technology

The context for design, management, creativity, innovation and business has been revolutionised by information and communication technologies (ICT). Digital computing is now fully embedded into the software, hardware, infrastructure, behaviour and flow of our daily lives. Globally, emerging technologies and technological innovations are impacting upon the structure of organisations at all levels, and changing how they interact with and enable new relationships, audiences, processes, practices and forms of engagement. This, in turn, opens up diverse opportunities for the design, delivery and management of these interconnected systems of people, products, services and experiences.

Law

Organised communities uphold and enforce particular rules and codes of conduct with an authority we refer to as 'the law'. There are different legal systems for every country, but in general, the purpose of law is to get people to honour the needs and welfare of others. The legal system exists to allow for the defence of justice, in law courts and legal cases, with guilt or liability being proved or disproved by the presentation of evidence by lawyers.

There are two types of law: common law (laws of tradition or established custom, revisable by judges); and statute law (legislation established by acts of parliaments, congresses and legislatures). Within statute law, there are two main sub-categories: civil law (for upholding the rights of the individual, initiated when one party takes out a grievance against another); and criminal law (for dealing with harmful actions through punishment, such as fines or imprisonment).

All individuals and organisations must recognise and conform to the legal framework; however, what is legally, ethically, socially or culturally acceptable practice in one location may not be in another. What constitutes gift giving in one culture, for example, could be interpreted as bribery in another. Since lack of awareness of local laws is not an adequate defence against such a charge, it is important to gain some familiarity with behavioural and cultural differences to minimise the risk of such eventualities.

Society, politics and environment

Organisations that take business ethics or Corporate Social Responsibility (CSR) to heart within their management structures and product and service offers are able to offer customers clear evidence of how business can benefit society and the environment, and influence local and global political agendas.

Equally, with the rise of technology-enabled communication platforms, whole communities can now question, influence and affect change, through 'bottom up' forms of social and political activism. In terms of design, sustainability – thinking for the long term – and sustaining prosperity is increasingly evident; for example, in the 'Cradle to Cradle' approach, which calls for a 'transformation of human industry through ecologically intelligent design' (McDonagh and Braungart, 2002). McDonagh and Braungart are optimistic that 'an industrial system that "takes, makes and wastes" can become a creator of goods and services that generate ecological, social and economic value'.

Society

People tend to organise themselves into groups that share distinctive beliefs, habits, customs and cultural activities. These shared beliefs, maintained over successive generations, result in the formation of lifelong or permanent groups known as 'society'. Social groups form around desires for companionship (family, villages), shared beliefs (religion, national loyalty) and the mutually beneficial exchange of services (trading, buying and selling).

In response to new and changing conditions, each generation seeks to protect the interests of their society so that they can live peacefully, comfortably and beneficially. How do we protect existing traditions and adapt to external challenges? How do we balance conformity with individualism? How do we safeguard the interests of both rich and poor?

Politics

The Classical Greek philosopher, Plato (428–348 BC) argued that all conventional political systems were inherently corrupt; while Aristotle (384–322 BC), a student of Plato, conversely saw politics as the relationship between the state and its citizens, believing that a truly ethical life can only be lived by someone who actively participates in politics. In a later historical period, during the Renaissance, Machiavelli concerned himself with practical politics: how to behave in any group interaction to attain and retain power – using coercion, manipulation and brutality.

1. Customers Who Care Campaigns put The Co-operative Bank's ethics into action, campaigning with customers on a range of important issues from climate change to trade justice.

The campaigns invited dialogue about key contemporary concerns in the areas of society, politics and the environment.

1

Politics is the process by which groups of people make decisions. Our choice of politics reflects our values and ethics: citizens vote for politicians and political parties who they believe will challenge the status quo or work to make things better. Our governments – the social entities elected by citizens – create the policies, legislature and other regulations by which they govern society.

Is political power held by governments or by their citizens? New political models based on greater transparency are driven by increased Freedom of Information, the collaborative activities of pressure groups and popular use of social media.

Environment

In an increasingly interconnected world, action taken by businesses, government and communities frequently has wider implications – geographically, economically, politically, ethically and morally. Current environmental debates suggest that worldwide global warming, climate change, floods, droughts, pollution and poverty are a result of unhealthy and destructive business practices and consumption patterns.

This is driving a 'whole lifecycle' approach and more eco-friendly 'green' initiatives such as recycling, renewable energy, low-carbon living and green job creation.

Environmentally harmful practices are being tackled by governments (green legislation), businesses (corporate governance) and society (lifestyle choices and behaviours, social activism). For design, this means considering how we engage in behavioural and systemic change to encourage a more sustainable future and a better quality of life – for all – through engaging with people and places in better ways.

'Design for development' considers how design can play a part in the people-centred transformation of how we live, consume and function in a less resource-intensive manner, so making it easier for people to live longer, healthier, happier lives.

Market demands and user needs

In order for a business to exist, the business needs a market; that is, the opportunity to sell what it does or offers to people who want to buy, use or engage with what it does or offers. Market demand stems from individuals and organisations that want or need the goods and services on offer. If market demand exists, businesses and their competitors vie with each other to satisfy this demand.

'Marketing is the management process responsible for identifying, anticipating and satisfying customer requirements profitably.'
Chartered Institute of Marketing

Before entering a market, businesses carry out market research to gather market intelligence. They analyse market trends, consumer needs and the competition; all of which inform plans for distribution (how to reach customers), the marketing mix (product, place, promotion and price) and the projected costs, sales and profits. Only then do they decide if the business can profitably enter the market with a new product or service.

Market-led approach

Once a business has identified a market demand that they decide to meet through the creation of a product or service, design becomes a way to give form, function, differentiation and appeal to branded products, services and communications; in a way that is fitting for the demands of the market, the personality, promise and positioning of the brand – and any cost, time or material restraints that accompany it. This is a market-led approach.

Meeting user needs

Design-led approaches tend to let *user needs* (the needs of the user) dictate what new products, services and markets are created. The needs of people become the driver behind the design of new products and services.

This is where a latent need in the user is identified by exploring the experience of an everyday situation or scenario – real or imagined – with the involvement of users in the design process itself. In this instance, design becomes a way of generating, visualising and testing ideas for new product and service design concepts and experiences.

This approach is common in contexts such as public service design, design in developing countries and community, social or global design challenges. Design becomes the trigger for practical and often innovative solutions that address real human needs, not market needs.

1, 2. Design Directions from the RSA (the UK's Royal Society for the encouragement of Arts, Manufactures and Commerce) frames a series of student design briefs within the social context of real world challenges. The briefs advocate a research-driven, user-centred response within a social context, and can intervene in areas such as crime, security and health – and so demonstrate the power of design to make a difference in the world.

'I Am Here' (below right) was a collaboration between designer Alex Ostrowski and the Frenchay Brain Injury Rehabilitation Centre in the United Kingdom. The designer approached the unit to find a way in which his skills could 'bring about positive change', by listening to the concerns of staff and patients in order to formulate a response. Addressing the issue of patients' reorientation, they together devised a colour-based system to help patients build a more stable relationship with their surroundings while coping with post-traumatic amnesia.

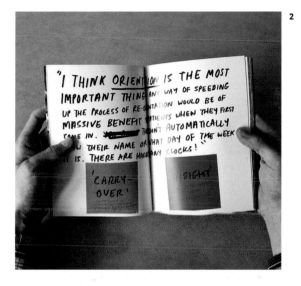

2

¹RSA

In this way, people become not just the generators of new products and services, but also of new forms of marketing (new types of marketing channels) – for example, social media and the 'word of mouth' acceptance of new products and services.

Opportunities for which a market is subsequently found to be viable are then developed into real products and services. This can reinforce an existing brand promise, or it can lead to the adaptation of an existing brand and even to the creation of a whole new brand to take the ideas to market.

'Crucially, good user-centred designers look at a problem from the point of view of the user, not the priorities of the system, institution or organisation. Designers observe people in context to understand the complex experiences, needs and wishes of individuals, and are able to represent and champion those needs throughout the design process.'
Jennie Winhall

Design audits, briefs and proposals

Clients frequently consult design experts in advance of actually committing to design projects, processes and initiatives. As in any new relationship, there will be a certain number of necessary initial conversations, in order to establish the suitability of both parties working together. But, in general, any consultancy work carried out for the client organisation should be charged for by the design expert, and not carried out 'on spec' in the hope of a future commission.

Some clients will have more design awareness than others, and helping clients scope out projects is a valuable step in both building working relationships and in developing live projects. Recognising the value of design means that design professionals must not take their expertise for granted by giving away their time and skills for free; similarly, clients must not take design expertise for granted by expecting to exploit a design professional's time and skill at no cost.

Hidden opportunities for design can exist in unlikely places. Conducting design audits, assessing and responding to client briefs, and defining design briefs provide the chance to promote a better (or more courageous) use of design.

The design audit

In general terms, audits are conducted to independently evaluate the performance of an organisation or part of an organisation – a system, process, product, person or project. Audits are usually conducted to establish and assure how fairly, validly or legitimately something is working. Auditors are usually brought into a company from outside – as they are independent of the organisation or system, they are seen as being more objective.

Design audits are carried out to assess the design capability of an organisation; to uncover how design is used (or not used) in support of the vision and values of the brand, the aims and objectives of the business model and organisational aspirations for the future. The audit reviews the use and performance of design internally (for example, in-house design teams and working conditions) and externally (such as products, services and communications), to ensure both consistency between what the company says (the brand identity) and what it does (employee behaviour, business practices or customer perceptions).

Diagram 1. When working with clients, PARK advanced design management use a 'project challenge audit' to analyse, prioritise and define project challenges, approaches and associated sub-projects (and methods).

1. First, a structured overview of the project is identified, and the content (what?) and process (how?) developed into a detailed project profile template.

2. Next (and before the actual start of the project), the project profile is defined and refined through audit workshops, pre-project scoping sessions and questionnaires with internal and external

stakeholders. Finally, the profile is used to explicitly specify the scope, focus and prospective challenges of the project, so that the brief can be defined and the right processes and tools utilised.

Diagram 1: The project challenge audit

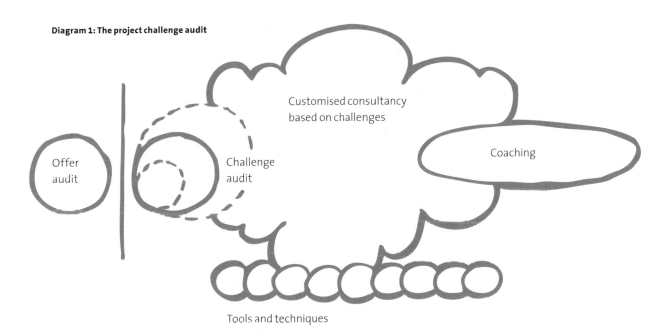

Offer audit

Challenge audit

Customised consultancy based on challenges

Coaching

Tools and techniques

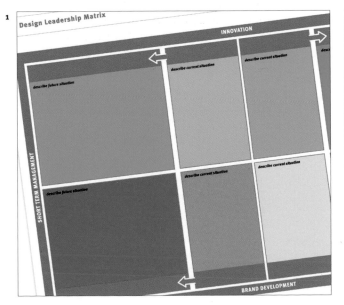

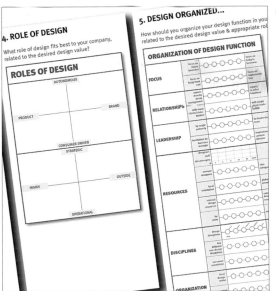

Table 1: Design audit process and report structure

Formal audit agreement

Definition: audit purpose and process

Market position, target audiences, competitive environment

Evidence of material collected

Review of the organisation 1: look, feel, behaviour

Review of organisation 2: stakeholder interviews (perceptions and aspirations)

Analysis of the use of design (including strengths, weaknesses, opportunities, threats)

Conclusion

Recommendations (and presentation)

Actions/next steps

Dissemination and circulation

The design audit is also an opportunity to suggest areas for enhancement. Evidence found during the audit process can be used to build the case for a more considered, intentional, creative use of design, both inside and outside the organisation. It can help set design agendas, influence the organisation's policies, shape strategy, set future design agendas and trigger new design budgets, recruitment, projects and practices. If the design manager carries out the audit with a diplomatic yet entrepreneurial approach, it is a valuable opportunity for design specialists to provide the support and expertise clients need to advocate the use of design.

The client brief

The client brief describes a particular organisational objective, initiative, project or task for which they would like to engage design expertise. The client brief may simply be a conversation that the client has with the design consultant about what they would like to achieve (to which the design consultant will later respond). When in written form, the client brief typically views things from the perspective of the client organisation's internal processes, targets, reporting systems and accounting deadlines. Therefore, the language employed in it can be quite analytical, numerical and to the point.

The first step is for the client to establish the client brief and to ensure that the design consultant understands what has to be done, by whom and when. Does the client need advice in developing the brief further? Has the client articulated the relationship between the client and their organisation, the brand and their audience, the business objectives and the proposed project, in a way that the design consultant understands? Putting the client brief in writing will clarify the specific aims, objectives, goals, deliverables, deadlines and budget available, and ensure that both the client and consultant can reach a common understanding of the requirements.

Good design practice involves questioning the assumptions that underlie a client brief. The opportunity for the design consultant is to use the client brief as the basis for a broad conversation to find out more about what the client would like to achieve, organisationally, professionally and personally. Discussing the brief will uncover hidden aspirations, expectations and limitations, as well as other potentially useful organisational objectives. The design consultant can also use this opportunity to verbally restate the brief in a way that raises awareness of latent possibilities or new approaches for bringing true creative thinking to the client problem. Spending time with the client, making them feel comfortable with the design process and proceeding in a professional, prepared and informed manner will increase the likelihood of securing a formalised and successful working relationship in the future.

Table 2: Writing the client brief

Introduction: project background, overview and opportunity identified

Company: the organisation, its brand vision and values, product portfolio, existing customers and management structure

Customers: target customers

Competition: competitors and their unique selling points (USP)

Positioning: the proposed strategy and plan of action

Design challenge: project objectives, scope of works, expected outcomes and specifications

Metrics for success: criteria for evaluation and for how success will be measured

Project plan: work stages, milestones, deadlines and deliverables

Budget: terms of agreement for fees, expenses and production costs

The design proposal

The design consultant considers, reviews and responds to the client brief with a design proposal. The proposal outlines the plan for what the design consultancy or agency will do for the client to creatively fulfil their business objectives. It will reiterate the client wants, needs and demands, and define the opportunity in a way that turns the ordinary into the interesting.

The design consultant possesses the knowledge and expertise of the most suitable design processes, practices and outputs needed to achieve the client objectives as set out in the client brief. It is important to ensure that this 'scope of works' is accurately described in the proposal in a way that encourages the client to want to commit to working with the design consultancy to achieve the best possible solution. Depending on the nature of the working relationship, it may also be the place to inspire the client to go further and consider other, perhaps more ambitious, options.

The design contract

Once the proposal for the 'scope of works' and the working process has been agreed, a contract for the engagement of the design services can be drawn up. As part of the contract, it is important to raise any potential legal issues with regard to, for example, intellectual property (IP) and copyright (who owns the work), non-compete (where the designer may not work with the client's competition for a defined period of time) and non-disclosure agreements (where project confidentiality must be adhered to). Clarification on the permitted use of publicity materials associated with completed projects will also be handled at this time. Once the terms of the working relationship are agreed and signed off, the work can begin.

The creative brief

The creative brief, written by the creative director in the design consultancy, is an internal document that translates the design brief and the design proposal into an internal working document for use by the design team. It is phrased in a way that successfully communicates the opportunity presented by the client, and challenges the design team to think imaginatively and creatively. It is important to ensure that there are sufficient materials available to inspire creative, yet still focused, thinking amongst the team. Has the creative brief articulated the relationship between the client and their organisation, the brand and their audience and the business objectives and the proposed project, in a way that the design team understand?

The scope of works

Depending on the size and scale of the scope
of works, there may be a single design team
(under the leadership of the creative director) to
whom all the work is allocated. Or the client project
may be broken down into a number of smaller
scopes of work, each of which is assigned to the
appropriate team. For example, the scope of works
may relate to the design team responsible for visual
language, the brand identity team responsible
for conceptualising brands, or to the information
architecture team responsible for customer
experience web development projects. In this case,
the appointment of a project manager is critical
to ensure the successful coordination of all the
different teams involved in the project.

'Good design can change society
for the better... it can inspire people
to demand good design.'
CABE

People

People form part of the 'human capital' of any successful vision, strategy or goal, and as such must be managed, valued and nurtured. Organisations are dependent upon people to make projects work. But the quality and the nature of the relationships between people can have an enormous impact on the success of an organisation's projects, as well as on individual stakeholder well-being and, ultimately, other business measures such as profitability and reputation.

Being 'people smart' and effectively managing relationships between different roles and resources, both in and across organisations, can therefore help facilitate project and business success. In an increasingly global economy, these relationships involve multiple stakeholders operating in 'value chains' that can exist across different companies, countries, suppliers and retailers. The importance of people in these value chains is not to be underestimated.

People dynamics – how people interact, contribute and are purposefully engaged – are the cornerstone of collaborative working processes and practices. Relationships between stakeholders can be complex and challenging, so understanding each of their roles and motivations can help in gaining insight into what drives their decision-making processes. In addition, for those involved in managing design, it also means that potential opportunities for creative collaborations and ways to create extra business value can be identified.

Increasingly, design management is concerned with how the relationships between clients, consultants and end users are organised and managed. This can influence how people create, lead and take part in the processes and systems essential to people working collaboratively and generating added value for business. Putting a managerial framework in place to deliver this added value is essential, as it is this framework that enables the collaborative creativity that allows businesses and designers to work together effectively.

Clients

People who commission, fund or otherwise support design projects are referred to as clients. Clients are responsible for communicating the strategic vision or direction of their organisation, both internally (for example, to other departments) and externally (for example, to design consultancies). They are ethically and financially accountable for the decisions they make on behalf of their organisation. Depending on the size and nature of their organisation, clients may have in-house design staff, and can also work with out-of-house consultants. Typically, they work with design consultancies to develop a project brief and plan of action that will deliver particular business objectives and results.

When commissioning design projects, a client's priorities are to achieve the highest quality at the best value for money possible, in a way that delivers results that both add value to their organisation and for their customers.

In the context of the creative industries, clients tend to view design in one of several ways: in terms of aesthetics (look and feel); as a process; as a response to users' needs; or (increasingly) as a strategic business tool. However, clients are continually looking for new business opportunities, and new ways to generate ideas and create value. This includes realising the potential of design and innovation as a means of differentiation and competitive advantage.

Currently, there is growing pressure for client organisations to take a more holistic approach to how they operate and the subsequent cultural, environmental, political and societal impact of their methods. Clients approaching the management of design and creativity in a strategic way tend to take a more long-term view of how value is created, realised and sustained. Design becomes a tool to enable potential business opportunities to be realised, in terms of how products, services and processes are developed.

Consultancies

A consultant – from the Latin *consultare* meaning 'to discuss' – has expertise in a specific area, and knows how to relate this expertise to a wider client context. Clients hire consultants for their expertise, and to help address organisational challenges or add value to specific projects. Consultants work independently or as part of a larger consultancy, and can be engaged for a short period of time or for long-term, ongoing client relationships. The benefits to clients of using consultants (as opposed to hiring the same individuals as permanent in-house staff) are that clients have access to deeper levels of expertise in a more cost-effective way – given that the relationship can be simply terminated upon project completion.

Currently, design consultants are eager to increase their influence across many aspects of an organisation, so as to encourage the use of design as a strategic business tool. For example, 'design thinking' as an approach can provide a way of dealing with the complexity of a particular situation, because the process of design is suited to engaging a range of different stakeholders, handling problems that are not clearly defined, and supporting fledgling ideas before they are fully formed. Effectively, design then becomes a way to secure further support, as it mediates between organisations, products and people. It is also a method for challenging preconceptions and assumptions that stakeholders may hold about possible solutions.

Because design, by its very nature, takes a people-centred approach to problem-solving, it is well positioned to enable a more integrative, holistic approach to addressing contemporary social, global, political and environmental challenges that exist in the world; and simultaneously realising new business opportunities – and sources of commercial value – for clients.

Design consultants are also a useful way for clients to gain an external perspective on their industry or markets. Consultants prioritise delivering to an agreed brief, on time and on budget, and providing well-designed solutions that add real, sustainable value to clients and customers alike.

Customers/end-users

Customers – people who buy or use a product or service to fulfil a particular need, goal or objective – can be internal to a client organisation (for example, another department), or external (for example, the public, other businesses, suppliers and even competitors). Customers typically view design as an experience that will fulfil (or exceed) their needs and expectations.

Both clients and consultants are also interested in the creative and innovative potential of engaging customers and end-users in the design process.

From a business point of view, clients know that collaborating with stakeholders in the process of creation can add value, reduce costs, achieve differentiation and competitive advantage, and still enable great customer experiences.

When design consultancies involve stakeholders in the actual design process, greater insights and additional perspectives are gathered at an early stage, resulting in a more thorough and 'empathetic' approach to the process of finding a design solution.

Because of the enabling and connected power of new technologies, companies are increasingly able to work within a 'network of innovation'. Customer and supplier relationships become 'conversations', value chains become potential sources of new ideas, and new products and services can be created 'in dialogue' with other people. Collaborative design (co-design), for example, is a way of developing products and services in partnership with multiple stakeholders, by capturing user-generated needs and, through the process of design, turning those needs into business propositions and design solutions. Design then not only enables the process of collaboration and engages customer participation; it also acts to give form and viability to new ideas.

1. Launched in New Zealand in 1994, Icebreaker was the first company in the world to develop a merino wool layering system for outdoor clothing. Each product reflects Icebreaker's core beliefs in honesty and ethics, evident in the way that they source materials, make products and operate as a company.

2. Working with a design agency, Icebreaker developed a brand identity; and a clear set of ideas around which to base the creative development of the offer. Icebreaker was the first outdoor clothing company to source only pure merino direct from the growers, which is handpicked, and then created into edgy, outdoor clothing that combines nature's work with human technology and design. © *Icebreaker Ltd*

Projects

A key factor in the success of design projects lies in how teams, processes and procedures associated with a project are organised, co-ordinated and carried out. We call something a project when referring to an endeavour that is in progress or about to be to be undertaken. Projects are broken down into work stages, each of which is executed until the project comes to an end. Typically, a project comes into existence because a client (internal or external to the organisation) has identified a particular user-need, customer demand or business opportunity, and decides to respond in a way that fulfils this need and also satisfies a particular client agenda, brand promise or organisational objective.

The client and the entity that will deliver the project (for example, a functional unit internally or an external consultancy) will agree a scope of works or a project brief that describes as fully as possible the aims, objectives, deliverables, key dates (milestones) and budget for the project. Depending on the nature of the project, this may be a very specific and defined agreement, or it may be a list of requirements that need to be fulfilled, even though the project outcome itself is as yet unknown.

The next step is to identify who will be involved in the project (the team), how and when actions will be carried out and decided within the project (the process), and what routine steps must be taken to accomplish the project (the procedures).

Beyond the definition of the project brief and the organisation of the project itself, it is important to anticipate and agree what criteria will be used to evaluate project success, so as to establish whether the project outcome meets these project performance measures (and is therefore a success). Successful design projects help add value and build credibility, for the team, for the organisations involved and ultimately for the process of design and the role of design management.

Teams: who will be involved in the project?

Teams are dynamic entities of people brought together for the life of a project and sometimes disbanded upon project completion. Depending on the purpose of the project, teams can consist of a variety of people: individuals, disciplines and business units inside an organisation; outside consultants and consultancies; supply and manufacturing partners; independent suppliers and distributors; as well as end retailers and customers.

In the delivery of projects, working effectively as a team is key. The decision to appoint a dedicated project manager is often dictated by the size and complexity of the project and the ability of team members to manage themselves and others. Each team member will have specific roles, responsibilities and duties to fulfil as individuals, and potentially additional codes of conduct, ethical standards and professional accountability associated with their own organisations.

Typically, teams that connect, function and deliver effectively reflect each team member's desire to contribute, in meaningful and mutually beneficial ways, to agendas that reflect shared goals and responsibilities, values and beliefs. Having a shared goal (for example, what is best for the customer), that still allows room for individual agendas (for example, career success) is one of the best ways to address differences between organisations and disciplines that could potentially create barriers to project success.

Processes: how will actions be decided and carried out within the project?

The term 'process' refers to the carrying out of a set of developmental actions and stages, which aim to progressively realise a particular end result. The steps taken are evolutionary, in that the project is achieved through the act of incremental (yet sometimes radical) change.

Processes can be standardised, customised or dynamic. Standardised processes are in effect procedures – that is, a routine set of instructions for how to carry out a task. We 'process' a complaint, for example, which follows a defined 'complaint procedure'. Customised processes are designed around the needs of a particular client, task or challenge. Customisation implies two parts to the process: first, the design of the process itself, and secondly, the carrying out of the process.

Dynamic processes acknowledge ongoing 'project change': change is a constant factor in some projects. Web 2.0 projects need dynamic functionality, for example, in the case of interactive web applications that are behaviourally responsive in real time. Therefore the process must be designed to be flexible, adaptable and interactive.

Within a process, decisions need to be made. What actions will be taken? What operations will be carried out? What end results (if they can be defined in advance) are to be achieved?

The management of design increasingly involves collaborative working processes; therefore, it is important to be aware of the actual dynamics that exist between people, projects and processes, and to keep track of how all resources can be purposefully and responsibly engaged to deliver value to customers. For example, process optimisation and so called 'lean thinking' dictate the need to consider how to achieve efficient and effective processes with the least harmful waste or damage possible (for example, by outsourcing processes or using ethical resources).

With regard to the value chain of design, there is currently increased demand for transparency and accountability in how 'supply chains' operate, to ensure that an organisation's processes and the resulting products and services truly reflect the values and beliefs of their brand.

'Whether one is a member of an organisation, a consultant to it, a supplier to it or a distributor, one owes relationship responsibility to everyone with whom one works, on whose work one depends; and who in return depend on one's own work.'
Peter Drucker

Procedures: what course of action or routine steps will be taken to accomplish the project?

Procedures are a set of instructions carried out in an agreed order to accomplish a defined task or activity. Procedures are set up by organisations to standardise a specific course of action. It is important to follow procedures as they are in effect agreements made about how particular activities and operations will be conducted.

Examples of procedures include formal documents and contracts for: buying or procuring resources; engaging design services; initiating and signing off projects and budgets; checking compliance with standards (for example, the International Organization for Standardization (ISO) or The British Standards Institute (BSI)); and selection criteria for working with partners, suppliers and manufacturers.

Procedures can define a physical task or the processing of paperwork. It is good practice for organisations to regularly review their procedures to ensure that they are still valid. Is there a better way of doing things? Are they up to date to reflect changes in company policies, government regulations and legal requirements? Have they taken into account feedback from customers or users?

A frequent criticism of procedures is that they inhibit creative ways of working. A design manager who can input thoughts during the creation or review of procedures can influence the criteria defined therein, in a design-friendly way. They may help an organisation to consider how to best balance the need for internally effective working controls and management practices, with the desire for creative processes that result in externally successful, high-quality design outcomes.

1, 2. Icebreaker have become a richly connected team of over 200 people in five different countries, and the company distributes to more than 2000 stores in 30 countries. The 70 staff in the global head office in Wellington manage in-house design, marketing (below) and product development; as well as driving the whole supply chain, which employs over 1000 people globally, many centred around Shanghai.

The actual 'supply chain' starts with the sheep. At Glenmore station, the merino's thick winter fleece is hand shorn by expert shearers who handle up to 170 sheep a day. Hardened steel blade shears (below, right) don't touch the skin and leave a thin coat of wool to protect the merino in case there is a cold snap.
© *Icebreaker Ltd*

3, 4. Shrek the merino sheep before and after shearing. Icebreaker maintains complete control over all the processes and selection criteria for manufacturing partners. Everything must meet strict business, environmental, ethical and societal standards, which guarantees that the company's environmental impact is minimised and that social ethics are upheld.

Products and services

One way that customers and end users touch, see and experience an organisation or brand in their daily lives is through products and services. Successfully getting product and service solutions to market relies on having solid structures, processes and systems in place to deliver a designed and managed customer experience. It is increasingly important to be conscious of the wider context of activities in which products and services exist.

In *Competitive Advantage* (1985), Michael Porter describes how a firm takes 'raw materials' which pass through a 'value chain' of activities in a particular order so that each stage (for example, design, marketing and delivering) contributes to the value of the final product or service, which eventually reaches a buyer willing to pay that value. The 'value system' is the larger interconnected system of multiple value chains and activities; for example, the company, suppliers, distribution channels and retailers. Porter suggests exploiting the upstream and downstream information along the value chain for opportunities to add value, either by performing activities more cheaply or more successfully than the competition (for example, by making improvements, eliminating costs or even bypassing intermediaries).

The actual design of the system is critical to the success of the product or service experience. How does a product or service connect to other products and services?

What systems are in place to deliver product and service solutions to the end user, in what location and by what method of delivery? What does the customer experience look and feel like at each stage? What is the best place to reach target audiences? Each of these stages can potentially be redesigned to create or add value to a product or service, and ultimately deliver that value directly to customers.

Porter (1985) describes how the value chain is a source of competitive advantage – the idea being to maximise value creation while minimising costs. In the global market, demands for more sustainable products and services are driving the need for changes in existing business processes, and also for entirely new business models and systems.

'Products exist in a vast environment of services, brands, cultures and competitors. But companies are realising that strategically designing products for the contexts in which they live can result in more imaginative, better integrated and ultimately more humane offerings.'
Steve Portigal

Systems: what networks, interactions and interdependencies are necessary for the effective organisation and eventual distribution of products and services?

System thinking involves creating a means by which a whole system can come together into a unified whole, so that the whole is greater than the sum of the different, interconnected parts. As such, the inter-relationships and interdependencies are as important as the individual parts themselves. The interconnections are often where the real opportunities for competitive differentiation lie, and their design should be carefully considered.

A system itself is usually set up in the form of a network, with the aim of distributing goods, services or experiences in an orderly, coherent and cost-effective manner. This may involve partners, collaborators, suppliers and end users, all of whom work together with a common purpose to help realise a vision and maximise value.

One way to add value is by reducing costs; for example, by streamlining or eliminating processes or by reducing inefficiencies within a system. Another way is to engage customers and suppliers so as to enable dynamic development processes that harness additional input at minimal cost.

Places: where do products and services originate from?

The Internet is revolutionising the way that people work together. Activities can be performed by sharing and distributing workloads between teams and functional units located anywhere in the world. Outsourcing – the 'sourcing out' of particular activities and functions within a value chain – allows organisations to gain external expertise while achieving cost savings internally. Potentially, any stage in the cycle of creation, production, distribution and delivery could be outsourced locally, regionally or globally, to where it makes most investment sense, in terms of business, society, technology and the environment.

The Value Chain Group has developed a value reference model (VRM) of the key business functions of a value chain. They are: research and development; design of products, services or processes; production; marketing and sales; distribution; and customer services. Different places are known for different areas of expertise, and business sectors such as the car industry operate with diverse business functions in different parts of the world – the goal being to leverage knowledge, expertise and cost savings inherent to particular locations.

The Internet is also transforming the supplier-customer relationship, and the connection between choice and demand. New models of mass collaboration and mass innovation are challenging traditional business models based on mass production (Leadbeater, 2008); as companies increasingly 'collaborate creatively', and innovate in dialogue with customers while being supported by technology (the Internet) and networks of suppliers.

The place in which an activity happens is often decided by cost, but locations can have different measures of 'worth' beyond cost decisions, based on merit and appeal, significance and meaning, and capability for creativity and innovation. It may be advantageous to engage particular places in the process of exchange activities that go beyond the buying, selling and production of more goods and services. Consumer trends within the food industry, for example, dictate that price and choice in food products is important to consumers – but so are other differentiators such as origin, variety, environmentally responsible processes and methods of production.

'The most market growth is not actually in the creation of new products, but in their exploitation, distribution and trade.'
John Howkins

Delivery: how do products and services get to people, places, audiences and end users?

Supply chains and production and distribution networks deliver products and services to end-users. But different audiences are reached through different channels, and the way in which products and services are received and accepted is part of the success or failure of the customer experience – and dictates whether they are compelled to engage or buy. A seamlessly designed and managed brand experience, delivered to a customer in a coherent and integrated way, relies on an understanding of how to orchestrate all the different delivery channels involved. Design thus becomes a useful tool to make business visible – in the products and services themselves, but also in the surrounding processes, systems and places.

'Touchpoints' describe all the ways that a brand, product or service can literally 'touch' or 'be touched by' people. Wally Olins talks about the four ways in which brands can express their core idea – through products, environments, communication and behaviour – so that the brand story makes sense across all channels (Olins, 2008). The point of taking a coherent, thoughtful approach to the design of touchpoints is that the quality of the experience that the customer has with the product, service or environment can be managed in a way that makes sense for the brand or organisation, and also makes sense to the customer or user.

1. Icebreaker's Baacode is a revolutionary system enabling customers to trace each garment back to the sheep stations where the merino fibre was grown, pictured here. A transparent supply chain is a core part of Icebreaker's philosophy, and the whole design of the business demonstrates this – starting from the growers and continuing through every step of the supply chain.

1

2

2. The Icebreaker ethos – respect for nature, ethics and sustainability – is reflected in the commitment to ensuring the purity and authenticity of every product, enabling users to trace their garments back to the farms that produced the wool they're made from, as this ad campaign states.
© *Icebreaker Ltd*

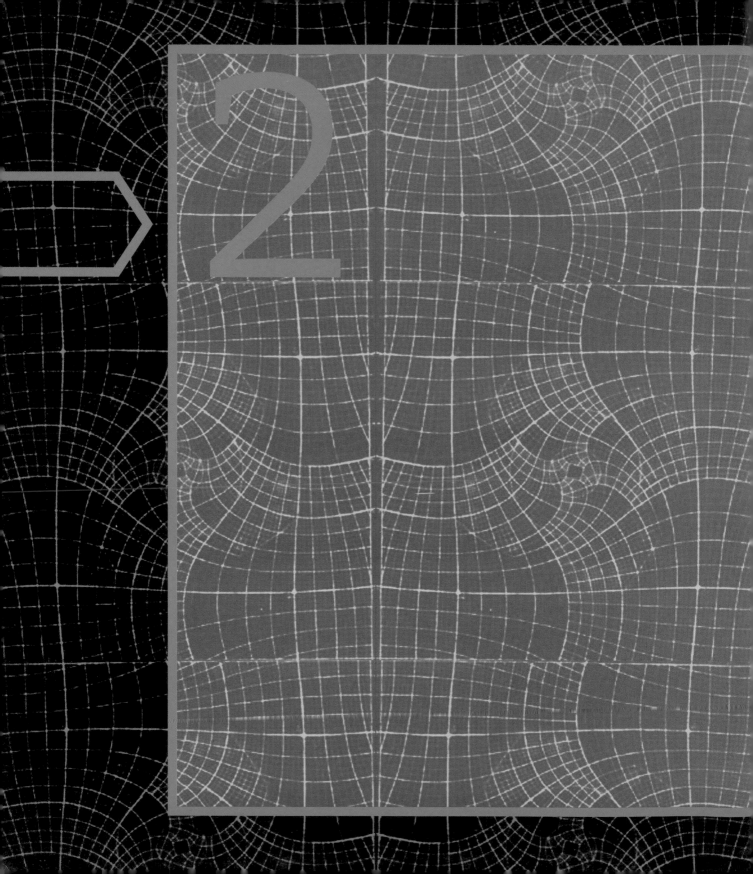

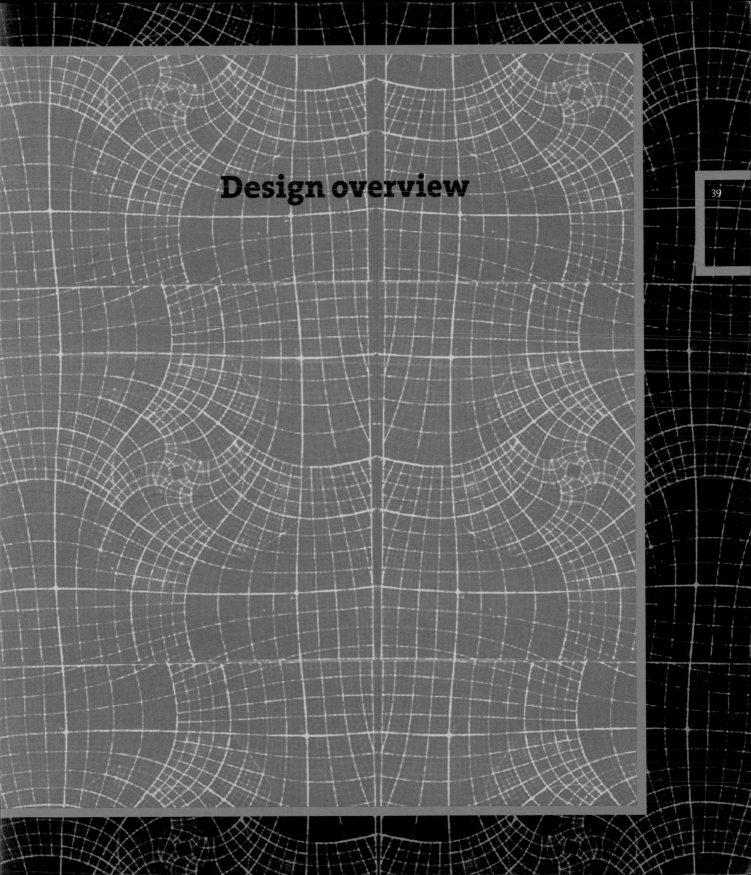

Design overview

The power of design

1

Supermarine Spitfire
Designed by RJ Mitchell

Mini Skirt
Designed by Mary Quant

Mini
Designed by Sir Alec Issigonis

Anglepoise Lamp
Designed by George Carwardine

Concorde
Designed by Aérospatiale-BAC

K2 Telephone Kiosk
Designed by Sir Giles Gilbert Scott

Polypropylene Chair
Designed by Robin Day

Penguin Books
Designed by Edward Young

London Underground Map
Designed by Harry Beck

Routemaster Bus
Design team led by AAM Durrant

Design exists in a wide range of contexts linked to society, the environment, technology, politics and economics. It is highly influential when used in the services of marketing and branding and is emerging as a compelling means of stimulating innovation in a variety of business contexts. Although there are some broad concepts, processes and skills common to all design disciplines, each specific discipline will of course follow its own explicit and highly refined process.

Design as catalyst

Design is both a noun (an outcome) and a verb (an activity). The 'outcome' of a design project can be seen in the products, services, interiors, buildings and software processes that we come into contact with daily. The 'activity' of designing is a user-centred, problem-solving process. Whether an outcome or an activity, design needs to be managed in order to ensure that the results desired are actually achieved.

Design is concerned with how things look and feel, but also with how things function and operate. 'Almost every design involves some balance of appearance and function, from the vases of ancient Greece to the latest status-symbol car' (Clark and Freeman, 2000). Design manifests itself in both iconic signs and symbols within culture, society and our own personal identity. It is the visual, aesthetic and expressive medium of artist-designers, as well as the generative process behind many discoveries, inventions and innovations.

Design is a problem-solving process (for example, to make life easier) as well as a problem-seeking process (for example, to discover hidden needs). It can influence behaviour, transform problems into opportunities and translate routines and procedures into unique, value-adding creative processes. As such, design is a catalyst for change.

1. In 2009, Royal Mail, the UK's postal service, issued the British Design Classics stamps (facing page) to celebrate a century of British design and honour some of the country's best-loved designers. The stamps feature instantly recognisable design icons from the 20th century and enable the 'Best of British' to be both showcased and sent around the world.

Championing design

People who lead, manage and harness the power of design learn to connect across different disciplines, cultures and organisational boundaries. They facilitate, engage and enable communication and collaboration between many different kinds of people. A design manager believes in the power of design; they can see the potential for design as both a form-giving solution and a catalyst for change, and therefore have the conviction and tenacity to make a case for design agendas.

Achieving high standards of design quality requires strong design leadership – so-called champions of design. CABE (the Commission for Architecture and the Built Environment) is currently leading an initiative to embed 'design champions' throughout industry and government, in all public bodies that have a responsibility for delivering and managing the built environment.

The purpose of a design champion, according to CABE, is 'to provide leadership and motivation, ensuring that every relevant organisation or project has a clear vision and strategy for delivering good design'.

2. Hug Salt and Pepper Shakers, designed by Alberto Mantilla: functional and charming, the design has universal appeal. Rethinking the shape in terms of geometry and ergonomics has additional storage benefits: the two figures embrace each other to appear as a single unit. The shaker holes form eyes, and the bold use of black and white symbolises yin and yang. *© Design Museum Shop* <www.designmuseumshop.com>

2

Design and society

We are, literally, surrounded by design, in the culture of everyday life and in the communities, objects and spaces we come into contact with every day. Design reflects the time we live in; therefore, what and how we design changes.

There will always be a market for products and services that are wanted and needed, that make the world a better place, that make life easier. Some of these wants and needs are marketing-led; others are part of wider social trends and concerns, such as increased health-awareness or a growing fear of crime. These are areas where design can play a part by visually and conceptually inquiring into such issues as: how can we design wellness and trust into society? Increasingly, we have to address the use of new technologies, global connectivity and the growing concerns about design for society, and design by society.

Design for society

Design for society is evident in initiatives such as 'Designing for the 21st Century', which examines the context in which designers create products, experiences and environments, and the role of technology as a creative enabler for new forms of product and service offers. New pressures on business and society demand design responses that take into account both the local and the global nature of highly interdependent and complex challenges. Social responsibility initiatives, in particular, are useful organisational tools to build positive relationships with the external environment – and to find socially beneficial opportunities for design. In the words of Hartley and Palmer (2006): 'commercial companies must take account of society's values because if they do not, they may end up isolated from the values of customers.'

Design by society

Design by society addresses the issue of how we engage users in the design process; for example, in participative design techniques such as co-design. 'Customers, users and stakeholders are no longer passive recipients of design; expectations are higher, increased participation is often essential' (<www.design21.dundee.ac.uk>). Today's societal challenges are the inspiration behind the new business models and opportunities set up by social entrepreneurs and driven by the power of social networks.

**Diagram 2: Abraham Maslow's
'The Hierarchy of Needs'**

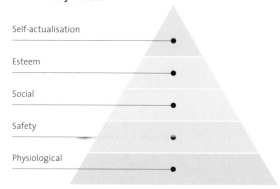

Self-actualisation

Esteem

Social

Safety

Physiological

Diagram 2. The Hierarchy of Needs (facing page) illustrates Abraham Maslow's belief that people aspire to become self-actualising, in other words, to fulfil their potential. His views on human potential have been vastly influential in our thinking on the nature of society, the value of work and what motivates human behaviour.

1, 2, 3. Encouraging healthy eating: in the United Kingdom, the Food Standards Agency had an ongoing campaign to encourage teenage girls to improve their diet and live a healthier lifestyle. Bell (<www.belldesign.co.uk>) was asked to develop the publicity, promotional material and merchandising to support a sponsored soccer tournament. The solution was 'Eatwell', a fresh, fun, new brand with the slogan of 'love yourself' and an associated PR campaign and website.

1

2

3

Design projects

Projects do not exist within a vacuum. All projects exist within a context that provides opportunities, as well as constraints and limitations. Both the constraints and the opportunities are triggers for, and sources of, inspiration for designers. What first appears as a disadvantage or a limitation often contributes to the uniqueness of the eventual solution.

Addressing challenges

Design is a problem-solving process for the practical and creative resolution of particular challenges. Design is as much about 'problem-solving' as it is about 'problem-seeking', as many needs are implicitly hidden, not explicitly revealed, and need to be uncovered. The role of the designer is to imagine a better way of doing things, to uncover the problem as well as search for the solution through the process of design; and finally, to communicate this future vision.

Once the design problem has been identified, the process of idea generation and addressing the opportunity through design begins. The design process itself may need to be 'designed'; that is, the approach and methods appropriate to the discipline and the media are decided. What form will the design process take, and what design skills will be required?

At this stage, the design team are selected and material provided that will inspire, excite and engage them. Are there relevant locations to visit? Should the users be observed, interviewed or actually involved? What about talking to manufacturers or service providers? What market research is available? In *Designing for People* (1955), Henry Dreyfuss points out that the designer needs to be: 'a keen observer of public taste [who] has painstakingly cultivated [their] own taste. [They have] an understanding of merchandising, how things are made, packed, distributed and displayed.'

Design thinking

This very early stage of a project is the time to engage 'design thinking' in the problem-solving process. Tim Brown, CEO of design consultancy IDEO, comments that: 'since design flavours virtually all of our experiences, from products to services to spaces, a design thinker must explore a "landscape of innovation" that has to do with people, their needs, technology and business' (2008).

Although some design problems can trigger completely new and original solutions, most design solutions are based on modifications of existing precedents – for example, the recognisable form and function in the shape of a chair or a cup. It is, therefore, important for designers to learn from what has worked before, and not invent a new solution just for the sake of being different.

1. Dutch design agency Ping Pong use cards to creatively explore 'what if' scenarios with clients and stakeholders, to get them engaged in and thinking openly about the challenges presented and opportunities available. Exploring ideas in an open-minded way during early stages of projects helps to spur dialogue and debate.

2. Arup is an independent company of designers, planners, engineers, consultants and technical specialists. Their Foresight Team created a set of cards identifying the 'Drivers of Change' that affect the future – in energy, water, climate change, waste, urbanisation and demographics. The cards are used as tools to facilitate workshop discussions about design – and to inspire new ways of thinking about design problems.

1

Enter the realm of the possible. There are no limitations.
Anything goes.
Take your idea and run with it. **Remember: everythings possible.**
Describe your idea within this newly imagined context.

Fact: It is estimated that one edition of the New York Times contains more information than a person in the 17th century would gather in a lifetime.
Back then, the advent of publishing brought about a great increase in reading material, though vast numbers of people remained illiterate.
What if your target audience was illiterate? What would your idea look like then?

Imagine a collaborative effort between your company and Dominoes pizza.
What are the possibilities?

2

The design process

Design is an iterative, cyclical, non-linear process. It is a decision-making series of 'feedback loops' of creative inquiry that refine each successive 'iteration' with the goal of reaching a design solution.

Design disciplines

Designers work both individually and in teams, in both single discipline and multiple discipline (inter-disciplinary) groups. They can and do need to operate in moments of quiet reflection and analysis, as well as in collaborative teams that lead to bursts of sudden insight. The process is carried through until an end solution or portfolio of solutions, such as products, services, environments or communications, is achieved. The solution must fulfil the requirements and criteria for success as outlined in the brief.

Different design disciplines have distinct design processes and methodologies appropriate to their discipline, objectives and outputs. Within the design industry, consultancies tend to differentiate their design services and stages so as to present a 'unique' process offer. By looking at the creative process in general, however, it is possible to identify some aspects common to all design processes and disciplines. The fundamental core of the 'creative process' is characterised by the following stages, as outlined by Csikszentmilyi, 1996.

Preparation: immersion in a set of problematic issues that are interesting and arouse curiosity.

Incubation: ideas are churned around, below the level of consciousness, and unusual connections are made.

Insight: pieces of the puzzle begin to fall into place.

Evaluation: deciding which insight is most valuable and worth pursuing.

Elaboration: turning the insight into something real.

Design methods

As a way to inform the design process, designers take into account the unique needs of the users for whom they are designing, as well as the production processes necessary to get the design to market. There are various methods and approaches that can be taken to learn more about user needs: shadowing or observing users in action; ethnographic methods (such as watching users in their own environmental context); and documentary design research via photo-journals and diaries. Talking to manufacturers can provide inspiration about the use of materials or production processes. The insights gained in the process of letting consumers/users and producers/manufacturers inform their thinking inevitably inspires more unique and creative solutions.

1, 2, 3, 4. Smart Design creates products and services that achieve relevance to consumer needs and desires. Their 'Smart Thinking' has led to some enduring philosophies that inform their design processes.

Smart Design's Smart Thinking on Addressing Gender: understanding how women and men evaluate products differently can result in designs that are better suited to all consumers' needs.

Smart Design's Smart Thinking on Considering Age: sensitivity to peoples' differing physical and cognitive abilities – whether young or old – results in design that is truly universal.

Smart Design's Smart Thinking on Humanising Technology: easy, natural, and instinctive interactions build meaningful experiences, giving products lasting value.

Smart Design's Smart Thinking on Understanding Emotions: deep connections with consumers are critical to the success of products and to the staying power of their brands.

Design skills

Designers are skilled in communicating the process of design, to solicit stakeholder feedback and secure client approval to proceed. They are also skilled at communicating what the final design solution will be like – experientially, aesthetically, visually and functionally.

Visual communication

The ability to communicate – visually, verbally and in writing – forms the critical common ground of any endeavour involving people, and is vital to successfully engaging clients and securing the resources, time, energy, advocacy, belief and commitment needed to see a project through to completion.

Using the right visual language to frame these discussions is one of the hidden opportunities of designing communication – the practice of communicating ideas through visual language in order to convey a message. Visual communication involves telling a story, compellingly, in words, images, graphics, colours and text. The language we use, the visual language we create, and the format in which we present our ideas are all enormously influential in how a story is received by an audience, and whether the story captures interest, gains support and is ultimately accepted, or rejected. Designers operate in business as both 'facilitators' of other people's ideas and conversations, and as 'design thinkers', taking a tangential, problem-solving approach to the challenges faced by business, society and the environment.

Design prototypes

A large part of the design development process involves 'prototyping' – the making, modelling or 'mocking up', in tangible or visible form, of particular stages of the design process in order to think about the design idea further.

Prototypes can range from hand-drawn conceptual visualisations ('paper prototyping', which is quick and cost effective), to computer-generated 2D or 3D images, to scaled or full-size physical models ('rapid prototyping', which uses digital technology to create 3D physical models with precise materials, surface finishes and design specifications).

Prototyping is a vital part of the design process, in that new ideas can be tested, evaluated and optimised, before committing budgets and resources to final (and costly) delivery stages. Although there may be several alternative solutions generated at an early stage in the design process, usually only one solution is taken forward for further development – the optimal solution that meets (or exceeds) the requirements of the brief, the needs of the stakeholders and the predefined criteria for success.

Prototyping is excellent for convincing a client of the merits of (and the business case for) the design, and for securing the involvement of those critical to the success of the project – whether because they have, for example, specific technical expertise to offer or critical financial support.

1. Dyson is about invention. The process of invention is a long and iterative process, trying something over and over again, changing one small variable at a time to improve the final design through thinking, testing, breaking and questioning.

2. As part of the design process, prototypes and new machines are tested in labs and home environments for qualities such as durability and reliability. Carrying out months of repetitive and rigorous testing is a lengthy process, but one that results in continual improvement. The semi-anechoic chamber is used during development to measure how much noise a vacuum makes.

4. Dyson designed a range of compact and lightweight cleaners that are ideal for aging populations and homes with limited storage space. The Dyson DC24 sits on a ball and turns with ease – providing greater manoeuvrability than standard cleaners. The motor sits inside the ball, making it lighter in hand and even easier to steer.

3. New product development starts with an idea that works. Dyson engineers often get ideas by trying out the ridiculous, which can spark extraordinary thinking. Many of the ideas they try are 'wrong', but Dyson believe that this is a good thing. Wrong ideas and new mistakes are incredibly valuable – they spark unthought-of possibilities and answers.

Design planning

Delivering design projects requires a plan of action. Planning is the process of deciding and organising how something will be done, before commencing delivery of the project. Design planning involves identifying how a project will be set up, managed and delivered; what resources are needed; and what actions will need to be taken, by whom, and when.

Project constraints

When planning the project, design managers need to establish some key facts. What are the strategic and operational objectives for the project? What project scope, outcome and criteria for success has been agreed? What timescales, deadlines and budget limitations are in place? If the key conditions are not realistic, then the design manager will need to consider renegotiating or aborting the project before committing to resources and setting up the delivery team for failure.

Project relationships

Inevitably, the results achieved in the final execution of a project are reflected in the thoroughness of the initial planning stages of the project. Project success relies on the combination of rigorous planning, good execution and careful consideration of the relationships and key decision-making processes between the client, the team and the project itself:

Client: Who is the project sponsor? The client contact? Has the contract, along with the terms and conditions, been signed? Is a confidentiality agreement necessary? How will payment of fees and expenses be handled?

Team: What skills are needed within the project team? Are the skills available internally, or are external skills required (sourced from, for example, professional recommendations or a design roster)? Where will the team work? At what frequency will team meetings occur?

Project: Are the roles, responsibilities and accountabilities of all project team stakeholders understood? Has a risk assessment been carried out? Have the resources needed for project delivery been fully identified and secured? Is the budget in place?

1, 2. Later design phases such as project planning are just as important as early concept design phases. Warsaw-based Robert Majkut Design studio completed the interior design for Moliera 2 boutique: home of the Valentino and Salvatore Ferragamo global brands in Warsaw. All Valentino boutiques worldwide meet strict brand and design quality guidelines.

Project planning processes typically fall into seven areas of activity (Young, 1997):

- Review the project definition
- Derive the project logic
- Prepare the initial schedule
- Resource and cost analysis
- Optimise and meet customer needs
- Validation and plan approval
- Launch the project

Ten reasons for project failure (Brinkoff and Ulrich, 2007):

1. Objectives not clearly defined
2. Participating employees not committed to project
3. Inadequate management support
4. Insufficient trust between partners
5. Project leaders lack integrative skills
6. Problems dealt with too slowly
7. Progress not consistent
8. Too little communication with partners
9. Weak teams – often 'miscast' or wrongly chosen
10. Conflicts with partners not solved constructively

Project management

Once projects are planned, they need to be managed – typically by a project manager. Project management is about planning and coordinating the resources necessary to get a project built on time, within budget and to defined standards of quality. It involves the co-ordination of the financial, material and human resources needed to complete a project and the organisation of work that the project involves.

Managing projects

Managing projects involves the balancing of three criteria: time (the schedule), cost (the budget) and quality (the performance). Most projects prioritise one or two of the criteria (for example, time and quality over cost, or cost and time over quality). However, for satisfactory project completion, these three criteria must balance; how they balance will affect whether the project is considered a success or a failure.

The Association for Project Management (APM) defines project management as 'the process by which projects are defined, planned, monitored, controlled and delivered such that the agreed benefits are realised'. APM breaks down the process into four stages:

Project organisation: prepare project brief; establish project team requirements, their working methods and performance measures; specify resource requirements; develop outline schedule; identify activities, procure project resources, agree contractual conditions, review tenders.

Project breakdown structure: develop detailed schedule (the exact sequence and timing of activities); secure project resources; identify and agree procedures (how tasks will be performed).

Project phasing and planning: manage team performance and responsibilities (who will do what); review project progress; comply with regulatory requirements, review and monitor finances and financial controls; monitor and adjust the project plan; manage the project team; maintain communication with project stakeholders; co-ordinate, monitor and control project schedule.

Project risk: risk awareness; controlling risk; risk management.

Diagram 3. The three influencing factors of any project are time, cost and quality, and it is the relationship between these factors that is of key concern to a project manager. Clients all have different priorities, and any conflicting demands must be balanced and managed within the project so as to maintain overall integrity of the final result.

Diagram 3:
The three key
project factors

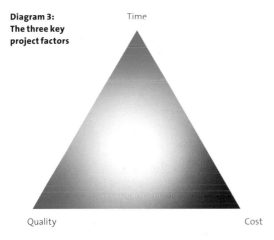

Time

Quality

Cost

Project management tools

To achieve the goal of a successful project outcome, project management tools help the project manager to organise their time more efficiently, to sequence, order and prioritise relationships, to manage risks against timescales, and to communicate the updated project status to the team and stakeholders at regular intervals. It also helps them to manage documents for accountability, reference and (potentially) legal purposes.

The project management plan (PMP) is the reference document for managing the project (APM 2009). Typically, this takes the form of a 'gant chart' – a reference document in the form of a bar chart or timeline, set up and used by project managers to plan, manage and deliver the project. Gant charts are created in software applications such as Microsoft Project.

1. Thorough project management ensures that projects are delivered through to completion, right down to the detail of the finishes; as seen here in Moliera 2 Boutique in Warsaw, by Robert Majkut Design (right). Appliqués similar to roses, inspired by the motifs on dresses, handbags and accessories have been reflected in the relief motifs on walls. High-quality stone, wallpaper and glass form sophisticated combinations of textures, colours and materials, following the guidelines of the Valentino brand. The 'Flore Cascade' custom-made chandelier is by British designer Sharon Marston. The project fulfilled the brief by honouring quality, the pre-determined style and global standards of the brand, while also creating design touches unique to the location.

1

Design success

Eventual project success must not only deliver to the brief, but must also satisfy and align with the business case, the brand vision and values, and the target market/target customers for whom the outcome is intended.

Evaluating projects

Project completion and handover is the final stage of the design project, and an important part of building a 'knowledge base of learning' for future projects and relationships.

Evaluating projects should include a project review and debrief with the client, the project team, and the actual users. Have stakeholder needs been met? How does the project measure up against the success criteria established at the start of the project? What benefits have been realised? It is good practice to carry out a closeout and archiving process of the project information, to ensure that documentation is accessible should it be needed in the future.

Measuring design value

Measuring the value of design is difficult because of the fact that its measures of success are easier to explain in qualitative terms (such as improved brand image, increased organisational learning, better communication), and not quantitative terms (for example, profits, units sold, market share increase). In addition, the benefits of design typically reveal themselves over time, not instantaneously (for example, through direct sales figures or increased profits). Deciding and agreeing performance measures appropriate to design, and building these measures into project goals and how success is evaluated, is one of the key roles for the design manager. It is also one of the most important ways to demonstrate how design as an activity can demonstrate a 'return on investment' in both financial and non-financial terms.

Table 3. The Design Management Institute (DMI) has listed nine ways to measure the success of design in business. These criteria can help in improving and measuring design's role in business performance. *(Lockwood, 2007)*

Table 3: Nine ways to measure the success of design in business

Purchase influence/innovation	Time to market/process improvement
Enable strategy/new markets	Cost savings/ROI
Enable product and service emotion	Customer satisfaction
Reputation/awareness/brand value	Developing communities of customers
	Good design is good for all/triple bottom line

Source: DMI, 2007

1. The iF Award is an internationally recognised mark of design excellence – a seal of product and service quality and a symbol of both good design and innovative, entrepreneurial thinking.

2, 3, 4. The Design Museum (below and below right) is the UK's cultural champion of design success, both in terms of modern design history and contemporary design innovation. Their exhibitions capture the excitement, evolution, ingenuity and inspiration of design, architecture and fashion through the 20th and 21st centuries. The UK's biggest provider of design education resources, the Design Museum acts as a bridge between the design community, industry and education (below, bottom right). The world's leading designers and architects are invited to participate in public events and exhibitions.

1

International Forum Design

2

3

4

55

Investment in design excellence

Design success can also be measured comparatively, by looking to benchmarks such as the competition, peer and press reviews, and design awards. As an example of how design awards evaluate performance, the iF concept award uses the following criteria: design quality; degree of innovation; visualisation of use/interface; target-group focus; tasks and objectives; degree of elaboration; social relevance/suitability; environmental compatibility; principles of universal design; choice of material; functionality; safety; usability.

It is important to remember that measurement of value is not always part of the remit of the design manager and their projects. Often, the decision to commit to a project has been made via return on investment (ROI) criteria that are part of a larger business decision or a more strategic business case. The key for the design manager, however, is to be the voice of design, and influence as best they can the perception of the value of design within the organisational framework.

Legible London: a new way of walking in the UK's capital city

case study

Legible London is 'part of an integrated transport information programme for central London, helping people plan and navigate their journeys no matter what mode of transport they choose'. (*Yellow Book*, 2007)

The system consists of 19 on-street signs, maps in bus shelters and signs in Bond Street Underground tube station, as well as paper area guides and audio maps. The idea is to integrate street information with tube exit directions, bus shelter information and a printed walking map, and to 'change the existing fragmented approach to walking information into a single, reliable, consistent and authoritative system' (<www.legiblelondon.info>).

The Bond Street area in the West End of London was chosen to test the prototype because of a commitment made by Transport for London (TfL) and the private sector to improve conditions and signage for pedestrians in the area. This busy area attracts Londoners, visitors and tourists with retail shopping, museums, galleries, hotels, restaurants and entertainment.

Walking in London

The aim of the Mayor of London's 'Walking Plan for London' was to make London one of the most walkable cities in the world: 'Walkers will be pointed in the direction of the area's main attractions. Unnecessary signage will be removed to leave the streets easily navigable by one recognisable set of information' (*Yellow Book*, 2007).

Information design specialists Applied Information Group (AIG), in association with Lacock Gullam, carried out the initial wayfinding study of central London as well as the design and final information system for the Legible London prototype. AIG specialises in developing and managing communications and identity programmes, and in creating and supporting information architecture both in the physical environment and with interactive media.

The wayfinding study found that there were 32 different pedestrian wayfinding systems used within central London. People often relied on the tube map to navigate their way around, which distorts people's perception of distances as they think it is too far to walk between stations. They also found that people are put off walking in London because they think walking is slow and complicated compared to other forms of travel.

1, 2, 3, 4. Funded by the City of Westminster, the Mayor of London and Transport for London (TfL), Legible London was created to provide a reliable, consistent system that provides better information for people who want to walk around the city (below and bottom right). 'The Legible London "walker" (bottom, middle) is instantly recognisable and derived from the universal symbol to represent walking' (bottom left) (*Yellow Book*, 2007).

case study

Environmental graphic design

The 19 new vitreous enamel and steel signs created by the Legible London scheme were planted in the streets of the West End of London, at strategic locations and intersections. A total of 46 objects were removed from the same area as their former function had become incorporated in the new sign design, thus helping to reduce street clutter. 'The replacement of redundant, unused information with a lesser number of useful designs improves the image of the street whilst reducing distractions for walkers,' according to Legible London's accompanying *Yellow Book*, 2007, which sets out the history of the scheme and the visual language it deploys.

A system of signs

As part of the new system, a 'family of sign types for walkers', based on the use of a map, was implemented. The monoliths (a wide, fixed sign containing wayfinding information) and the miniliths (a narrow, fixed sign containing wayfinding information) act as both area identifiers and route supports. They share common design conventions, which helps users both in becoming familiar with the design language of the wayfinding system, and also aids how they develop personal mental maps of the area. The design elements used include:

- The '**walker**' symbol, identified in a yellow strip at the top of the sign, and clearly visible from a distance.

- **Addressing** in a typeface, colour, and naming convention that is consistent with printed maps.

- **Directional information** to show the way to other nearby London boroughs, neighbourhoods and communities – referred to as 'villages' – or areas of interest, and to draw attention to nearby visitor attractions that may be out of sight.

- **A planner map** to orientate the viewer in terms of journey distance and time.

- **A finder map** indicating things within a five-minute radius and identifying local landmarks within eyesight.

- **A streetfinder** alphabetically indexed and referenced to the map.

Each new sign includes a consistent use of colour system, symbols, maps, street directories and directional plates, which aim to be as inclusive as possible for a range of different users and abilities (for example, people with minimal familiarity with the city, regular commuters, people with visual impairment, wheelchair users, or people whose first language is not English).

Design elements

Typography: AIG used Transport for London's typeface, 'New Johnston', as the identifying font – a font originally developed by Edward Johnston for the London Underground system in 1916. By using this existing font, AIG were leveraging the benefits of consistency and the familiarity people using public transport in London already have with this style of typography – which is embedded in the fabric of the city. Consultation with the UK's Royal National Institute for the Blind (RNIB) established that using a minimum font size of 12pt is desirable where possible and practical, to aid legibility for those with visual impairment.

All text is regulated to contrast clearly with the background colour (System Service Information Standard). Capital (upper case) letters are commonly used in the street signs and street name plates in London, and AIG chose to work with this existing convention as it is beneficial to speakers of languages with a non-Roman alphabet. The *Yellow Book* states that: 'these visitors may find it easier to relate streets on the map to street nameplates' (2007).

Colour system: The prototype signs and maps use high-contrast colours for optimum legibility: namely, either a dark blue background with white or yellow text, or a yellow background with black text. For print specifications, TfL colours are referenced using CMYK and the Pantone Matching System (PMS), whereas paint specification references are made to the Natural Colour System (NCS).

Pictograph symbols: The Transport for London pictogram standard, already in existence, was designed to provide a pictogram reference source for all transport modes within the TfL group. The pictograms are based on the British Standard for Pictograms, and are intended to be both clear in meaning and consistent in their design.

For the Legible London prototype, TfL's 'walker' symbol was used as the marque for the wayfinding signs. It is clearly visible from a distance. Symbols are especially useful for disabled people to identify where steps, ramps and disabled-friendly toilets are located (*Yellow Book*, 2007).

case study

Maps: The maps used in the Legible London prototype include details about the relationship between distance and time, so that people with limited mobility can better estimate how long it will take to reach a desired destination, and where convenient resting points may lie along the way to enable them to take breaks on their walks. Images of buildings in 3D act as a literal representation of buildings and landmarks, while making the reading of maps more intuitive (*Yellow Book*, 2007). Printed maps can be picked up in Underground stations, and users will find that the design and referencing is consistent with the prototype wayfinding signs.

Directional information shows the way to other nearby areas and visitor attractions that may be out of sight. The base of each sign indicates which direction is north through the use of an engraved arrow symbol. Street directories, or 'streetfinders', are alphabetically indexed and cross referenced to the map on the sign as well as to that on printed maps.

Evaluation methodology

Research undertaken before and after the installation allowed the benefits of providing high-quality map-based pedestrian information in the street to be measured, so providing clear evidence of its success. The project had three objectives: (1) to measurably improve public understanding of the area with information for walking, benefiting the local economy, the transport system and public health; (2) provide proof-of- concept to support TfL's business case for establishing Legible London as a flagship project; and (3) deliver a quality system that can be systemised for use throughout the capital, confirming the need for a pedestrian wayfinding system of this type.

A mixture of qualitative and quantitative methods were used, including 600 behavioural observations, 100 followed walks with task setting, focus groups and 2600 interviews. The nationally recognised Pedestrian Environment Review System (PERS) was the methodology used to assess and evaluate the quality of pedestrian networks. Measurable benefits were identified; for example, the fact that 62% of people stated that it would encourage them to walk more.

The 'Walking Plan for London' report recognised the need to create a safe, attractive and accessible environment that both improves Londoners' experience on the street and their attitude to walking. With the population of London projected to grow by 800,000 people by 2025, increasing walking journeys is an important way of helping to manage the demands this increase would otherwise place on an already-overstretched metropolitan transport system. These initiatives are also part of an ambitious plan to renew the West End ahead of the 2012 Olympics in London, as well as being designed to encourage visitors to venture off the beaten track.

The new system of signs, currently being extended to other areas of London, is transforming people's experience of visiting an area with many hidden shopping and alfresco dining gems, as well as one that is rich with layers of cultural history.

According to AIG, it is the largest coordinated pedestrian wayfinding system in the world, supporting a global culture change towards more sustainable use of our cities.

contextual perspectives

Sorena Veerman
PARK

Based in the Netherlands, PARK helps companies direct their internal design group or external design partners. Most of PARK's clients are design directors of mid-size to large manufacturing companies with an internal design function.

Design skills; methods, tools and processes

'Being *dedicated* to our clients and the profession. Being *persistent* in dealing with challenges and creating the right solutions for the long term, although sometimes this can be difficult. Being *surprising* with holistic and creative thinking and sharp visualisations. Being *true* and personal, in client relationships as well as company challenges.

'As a consultant in PARK I face many challenges. The above qualities allow me and my colleagues to work with the many different clients in the area of design management. We build personal relationships with our clients and help them deliver better products and experiences to their customers and users.

'I work on one–five year projects, during which I help companies to better organise and integrate design. This long time-frame is necessary to make sure that changes in strategies, organisations or processes are both developed and adopted by the client before we leave.

'Increasing the value of design by changing the approach of design, specifying the leadership role of design and ensuring a better integration of design and its processes often means the need for a culture change – and that does not happen overnight.

'To manage these projects, PARK defines four key phases: analysis, creation, development and implementation. Some projects encompass all phases, others only a few. For me, each of these phases has its own specific challenges. For example, in the analysis phase I have to collect relevant information, judge the importance of it and define the relevant links. My specific challenge, however, is to put the analysis in the right context as soon as possible. For instance, if I interview Grundfos business managers and project managers about managing design, the questions I ask steer the answers that I receive. I therefore have to consider my questions very carefully to be able to get relevant information.

'The creation phase is about defining the direction. My challenge here is to keep a holistic view of the company and first define the general solution that shows the big picture. Later, I use the development phase to dive into the details. In this development phase, I also have to make sure that I develop tools and materials that are relevant for the internal stakeholders.

'This said, my biggest challenge in general is to involve project stakeholders at the right moment and with the right approach. I need to start building relationships with key persons and create interest in the project already in the analysis and creation phase to be certain that I can fully use their knowledge in the development phase, and their energy in the implementation phase, without losing time or facing too much resistance.

'Internally, the PARK "toolbox" helps me to face these challenges in each phase. Our toolbox describes our everyday practices. These tools can be big, describing the development of a product design style, or small, describing ways to visualise workshop results or organise inspiring training workshops. The toolbox stimulates me to share knowledge with my colleagues and inspires me while managing client projects.

Sorena Veerman
Consultant at PARK
advanced design
management,
Netherlands

'Next to consulting work, I also run the PARK European Student Network, consisting of 15–20 masters students from design management programmes in eight European countries. The ESN students support PARK in conducting design management and research projects. I facilitate assignments and workshops within companies to help students experience real-life design management challenges, and the companies get fresh thinking from young design management professionals.

'Working with enthusiastic students who are full of new ideas is very refreshing and inspiring, and my coaching helps them to ensure a better fit between their ideas and the business reality.

'All these initiatives and projects, our various international clients, as well as our internal knowledge sharing, make PARK a very dynamic place to explore and exploit design management to the fullest.'

Wen-Long Chen
Nova Design

Nova Design is one of the largest independent design consultancies in the greater China region. Nova Design started out as a design studio in Taipei, Taiwan, and has expanded to more than 230 staff at six different branch offices worldwide across Sondrio (Italy), San Jose (USA), Shanghai, Xiamen, Taipei, and Ho Chi Minh City (Vietnam).

The design process: prototyping for innovation

'To run its global operation, instead of having each SBU run independently, as CEO and President of Nova Design, I took a different approach. Influenced deeply by the Buddhist theory of relativity, which states that everything is conditional, relative, and interdependent, I see managing discipline and freedom as a way to explore two sides of innovation. To have designers thrive in two seemingly different yet co-existent cultures, Nova Design encourages designers to focus on three key capacities: professional skills, resource integration, and knowledge value.

'To me, great design comes from managing innovation. Inside Nova Design, designers can advance themselves with their expertise, such as computer-assisted design skills, research analysis, or sketching skills. Outstanding skills contribute more to a design project when designers can integrate expertise from different resources.

'Finally, when cross-disciplinary paradigms and knowledge are added or incorporated to better a design, the designer with such a capacity advances to the managerial level inside Nova. They can then help shape the strategy of a design project.

'Throughout its 20-year practice, Nova Design has transformed the product development process with a comprehensive, digitally based knowledge management system. Such a system helps turn tacit knowledge into explicit knowledge and considerably reduces the learning curve of each designer. In addition, it offers two ways to add innovation value to client product development in providing this accumulative database and providing a one-stop service to Nova's clients. This system is upgrading itself, along with the development of Web 2.0. In China, there are more than one million students registered at design schools and more than 200,000 graduates each year.

'During my frequent visits to design schools in China, I observed that this vast growing force of design will change the way that design is executed in the global marketplace.

'Unlike the conventional way whereby users represent the demand and designers align themselves with the suppliers of the market, in the near future, users may soon be participating in creating products, too. Such a process will be more open and democratic, where the value of design becomes about providing and executing integrated solutions.

'As designers evolve from occupying a skill-based role to becoming a solution provider, the concept of design will change, too. It is therefore inevitable that a revolutionary transformation will take place in the design education of China. Already, a more dynamic design culture is being observed all over China.

'Take the latest 2009 Shanghai Auto Show, for example. Not only is it the third largest auto show in the world, it also made China the world's number one auto market. Major Chinese auto manufacturers also took this opportunity to show off concept cars developed by their in-house teams. Among them, Geely's concept car, Intelligent Geely, grabbed the attention of the international media. Some even commented that this IG may be a potential competitor against the Smart car.

Wen-Long Chen
CEO and President,
Nova Design, China

'The design focus of the Geely IG concept car is to target those who enjoy Shanghai's urban lifestyle. Sustainable design thinking plays a big part in the design of the car; one of the unique features is the three-seater layout, which places the driver's seat and steering wheel at the front-centre with two full-sized seats and one child-seat in the back. This three plus one design accommodates both the left-hand/right-hand drive markets and significantly increases usable interior space.

'This was the first project accomplished by Geely, a Chinese auto maker, and Nova Design. Nova initiated an internal project "design hive" when designers from Taipei, Shanghai, and Sondrio (Italy) worked side by side utilising web-based brainstorming sessions to come up with, explore and gain feedback on concepts. This was followed by clay modelling, reverse engineering, master models, and ME design. Computer-assisted methods (CAID/CAD/CAM) were applied for design modification in real time between Sondrio (Italy), Taipei and Shanghai.'

Dr Miles Park
University of New South Wales, Sydney, Australia

contextual perspectives

If product design is to become more useful, usable and successful in meeting people's changing and evolving needs, it needs to understand user-behaviour. Learning from examples of user-generated content, open source and user participation in online environments, adaptive design is an approach enabling design solutions to become contextually relevant, situationally specific and inherently reconfigurable by the user.

Design planning: adaptive design

'The traditional activities of product and industrial design have broadened and diversified from the role of devising product forms and detailing for manufacture. This shift of focus includes not only the design of physical products, but also the design of services, experiences and even business practices. Firms such as IDEO have become well known for incorporating user-observation and user-participation techniques into the design process, adopted from fields such as Anthropology, to better understand the needs, experiences, behaviours, perceptions and aspirations of users.

'By better understanding user-behaviour, design can become more useful, usable and successful in meeting peoples' needs and can also lead to new innovation. For industrial design, this offers new opportunities to work for clients in sectors of the economy that traditionally do not use design in such a strategic setting, including non-profits, social enterprises and service sector areas of the economy. Again, IDEO offer instructive case studies such as their "Keep the Change" project for Bank of America or "the blood donor experience" project for the American Red Cross.

'Through applying new design techniques to understand user-behaviour come other opportunities for design innovation. One such area is the increasing interest in how design can be used to "guide" user-behaviour. By "designing-behaviour" it may, for instance, be applied to promoting sustainable behaviours through energy-saving devices that prompt behaviour change. Energy-use meters such as the WATTSON, designed by three RCA graduates, allows users to "see" the electricity they are using in their homes. This encourages the user to switch off unnecessary lights and appliances.

'Advancing the concept of guiding user-behaviour, new trends and practices are becoming well established on the World Wide Web (WWW). Coined as a term – WEB 2.0 – to describe a combination of elements, including user-generated content, open-source software and user participation, popular sites such as Flickr, YouTube, Facebook, Wikipedia and eBay all rely upon a perpetually evolving design architecture where the user creates the content. For industrial design, this offers new opportunities for product innovation by enabling products to be adaptive by the user – to meet their individual circumstances and changing needs. The advantages of doing so can enable firms to create a closer relationship with their customers, enable a better product-fit to the user and help prolong product life-spans, especially in fast-moving sectors, such as consumer electronics.

'An adaptive product requires the designer to create a product that is intentionally "unfinished" or "open" to be completed by the user. The user becomes a co-producer in the design of a product, in a continual process that is contextually relative, situationally specific and inherently reconfigurable. This requires user-observation and testing techniques to be integrated into the design process in a two-way traffic between the designer and user.

Dr Miles Park
Senior Lecturer,
Industrial Design,
University of
New South Wales,
Sydney, Australia

'Informally, such activities are already taking place with many websites and magazines offering amateur design enthusiasts tips on how to reassign, reconfigure and hack products so as to "void warranties" and take control of their products. In the words of <Makezine. com>, "If you can't open it, you don't own It." In a formalised and strategic business setting, we are starting to see the application of these principles to interface design within computer and handheld communications devices where users can create, customise and change the way that they interact with such devices.'

Management overview

Economics

Economics is a social science that considers how the limited resources of the planet can best be managed to serve the unlimited wants of humankind. It addresses the business cycles and affairs of both individual nations and the world (so-called local and global economies) and is of fundamental importance with regard to how companies make decisions about business and finance.

Adam Smith, commonly referred to as the father of modern economics, described the incentives of self-interest and the common good as an economic driving force: 'Man, in pursuing his own economic advantage, is guided as though by an invisible hand (of competition) to serve the interests of society.' The Wealth of Nations (1776) identified 'the division of labour' (with strata of people performing discrete skilled tasks) as the way to increase 'the wealth of nations'.

The economic system

The 'economic system' describes 'the web of transactions that binds the economy together' (Heilbroner and Thurow, 1998). The forces at work are those of supply and demand: how we allocate, produce, distribute and consume the goods and services people want, and how we create the economic, social and moral incentives to which people will respond (Levitt, 2005).

Incentives strongly influence individual behaviour and preferences, especially in 'market economies' such as capitalism, where there is little government intervention or central planning and all economic and pricing decisions are based on the aggregate choices of a country's people and businesses. Suppliers manufacture or produce goods and services, thus creating supply, while consumers value the goods and services enough to pay for them, thus creating demand.

Economics operates on two levels:

Microeconomics relates to the supply and demands of people, companies and industries. It relates to how individuals, entities and markets interact under a range of varying conditions and regulations.

Table 4. A STEEP analysis can be used to help identify how changing circumstances and future trends in society, technology, the economy, the environment and in politics will affect the need for an organisation's current offers. Appropriate action can then be taken to satisfy anticipated demand for existing product and service offers, and develop new business ideas. *(Source: adapted from ARUP 'Drivers of Change', ARUP Foresight and Innovation)*

Table 4: STEEP Analysis: Predicting social change and future trends

Social	Technology	Environment	Economic	Political
Aging population	Biometric ID	Disposable quality goods	Consumer debt	Ethical investment
Education for all	Connected communities	Ecological footprint	Democratisation of luxury	Global governance
Future households	Energy infrastructure	Endangered species	Digital currency	Pensions
Holistic wellness	Radio frequency identification (RFID)	Energy and water use	Global trade	Surveillance society
Population distribution	Wearable computing	Urbanisation	Outsourcing	Trading blocs

The market, and the supply of goods and services, varies over time, thus so too do factors such as price and quality, depending on demand. Items in short supply usually command a higher price; and increased competition drives quality.

Macroeconomics is the area of economics which studies the behaviour of aggregate economies, that is, the economic activity at the country level and above. It tracks variables such as unemployment, inflation, and levels of saving, spending and investing. It also traces the flow of capital in and out of countries; that is, the Gross Domestic Product (GDP), a measure of the value of all the goods and services produced by a country.

The production of goods and services

The production of goods and services requires the existence of both a regular flow of wealth or disposable income (with which to buy and sell) and resources (with which to make things). Typically, these resources – referred to as the 'factors of production' – are land (natural resources), labour (people, both skilled and unskilled) and capital (tools, machines and buildings used in manufacturing and production). Entrepreneurs and enterprises bring these factors of production together to create an output – the actual products and services that people want and need. This demand is what creates the particular market for the output. The strength of demand for the products is such that people are willing to pay the market price.

Factors of production

Initially, businesses make decisions about how the factors of production are organised to produce the desired outcomes. Secondly, they will analyse the cost of production and their required return on investment (ROI). Relative to what the market will bear and to the pricing decisions of competitors, they will then set their own price.

Production can be supported by 'economies of scale' which describes the cost advantages of a company producing a product in larger quantities so that each unit costs less to make (Ivanovic and Collin, 2005).

Through the management process *and* the identification of constraints, trade-offs and risks, choices are made in order to add value. Provided the market desires this 'added value' and is willing to pay the market price, and provided the market price is greater than all of the costs associated with making the product, there will be a profit.

The process is a constant trade-off between risks. 'Firms must decide what to produce, how and where to produce it, how much to produce, and at what price to sell what they produce – all in the face of the same kinds of uncertainties that consumers have to deal with' (Wheeler, 2002).

Growth and economics

Governments, countries and regions that can successfully stimulate a culture of new business start-ups and growth enterprises can, as a by-product, also encourage increased employment, the creation of new jobs and higher income and spending levels.

Ultimately, the net effect will be to grow the overall economy. Economics is continuously evolving and new economic models such as the network economy, the knowledge economy and the creative economy are driving new organisational and business models.

In many cases, these new models are able to leverage the opportunities presented by advancements in technology and the effects of increasing globalisation.

Diagram 4: The progression of economic value

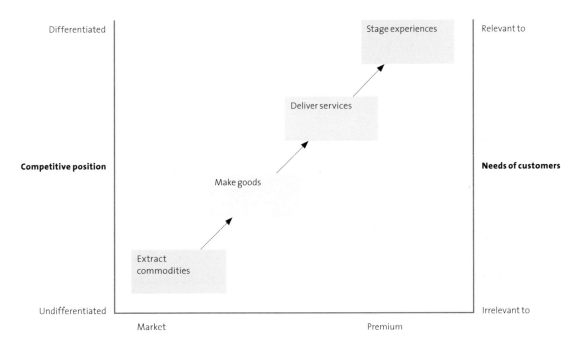

Diagram 4. This diagram illustrates the progression of economic value. Based on the evolution of the 'experience economy', each successive offering increases in value because the buyer finds each offer more relevant to what they truly want. Through differentiation of the offers – for example, through customisation – companies can charge a premium price based on the distinctive value provided, not on the market price of the competition. (*Source: Pine and Gilmore, 1999*)

Business and enterprise

An enterprise is a system for carrying out the activities of a business. Organisations that are set up to conduct business and enterprise activities exist within an external context (which generates their business idea, challenges and purpose), and an internal context (how they will take advantage of the opportunities available and achieve their purpose).

The business of business

According to Peter Drucker, the purpose of business is to create a customer; that is, identify a customer demand, then supply a product or service that satisfies this demand. The starting point for management is not the product or service offer, nor the market need, but what the customers consider of value and the incentives for their behaviours and choices (Drucker, 2005).

The 'core business' of a business is that which it was set up to do: what it does well, what its key knowledge and skills are, what makes it different from the competition and why it succeeds or fails. When considering how businesses could evolve, it is good practice to regularly evaluate this core business in terms of customers, key sources of differentiation, profit pools, capabilities and organisational culture (Zook, 2007).

The business idea and any associated products and services must be something that customers will value and pay for. The money invested versus benefits gained (cost-benefit analysis) must be justified.

Although all businesses are set up to make a profit – to sustain or grow themselves, and to satisfy shareholder demands for return on investment – every business also has a mission, vision and values that dictate how it operates; this gives the business meaning and purpose beyond financial gain, so as to, for example, benefit the broader context of society.

Typically, industry specialists have more expertise in key sectors, and the added value of designers and design managers is likely to be in how they provide fresh thinking, creative ideas and contextual perspectives that are outside the boundaries of the industry domain.

Diagram 5. In *Competitive Strategy* (1980), Michael Porter described the generic strategic approaches that companies could pursue when building competitive advantage, as illustrated in the table:

(1) Cost leadership – the low-cost leader; (2) Differentiation – differentiating from the competition through a unique feature or selling point (USP); (3) Cost focus – focusing on a narrow or niche market; and

(4) Differentiation focus – differentiating in a way that would not be easily imitated by rivals.

Diagram 5: Building competitive advantage

Type of competitive advantage

	1. Cost leadership	2. Differentiation
Broad target market		
Competitive scope		
	3A. Cost focus	3B. Differentiation focus
Narrow ('niche') target market		

Diagram 6: Porter's Value Chain Model

Margin

Organisational infrastructure

HR management

Technology development

Procurement

| Inbound logistics | Operations | Outbound logistics | Marketing & sales | Service |

Diagram 6. Porter's Value Chain Model is a systematic way to examine how competitive advantage develops and to identify where value is added in an organisation. The value chain is based on the process view of organisations, in which a manufacturing or service company is seen as a system made up of many sub-systems, each with inputs and transformation processes and outputs involving the procurement and consumption of resources. How well the value chain activities are performed determines the costs and affects profits.

Diagram 7. Porter's Five Forces Model is a competitive strategy framework showing the external factors that influence industry profitability.

It seeks to illustrate how competitive advantage can be achieved by incorporating industry conditions into the strategy and value chain of business operations.

The industry context

All businesses exist within an industry context of other organisations that compete directly and indirectly for people's time, attention and disposable income. In this 'competitive environment', businesses continually seek to gain competitive advantage, typically through differentiation (defining a unique position), or through pricing and cost decisions. According to Porter (1988): 'Competitive strategy is the search for a favourable competitive position in an industry, the fundamental arena in which competition occurs. Competitive strategy aims to establish a profitable and sustainable position against the forces that determine industry competition.'

Businesses developing new ideas are seeking an unsatisfied opportunity for a market demand or user need: gaps in existing markets or entirely new markets. They exploit new opportunities arising through changing circumstances – in society, technology, the economy, the environment or in politics – and position an offer to satisfy a current or anticipated demand. Competitive analysis can help to identify opportunities in the market. According to John Kay (1995), competitive performance is determined by the match between the characteristics of the firm and the challenges that the company faces. A SWOT analysis (which determines the strengths, weaknesses, opportunities and threats facing a market or company) can help generate ideas for new strategic directions and market opportunities.

**Diagram 7:
Porter's Five
Forces Model**

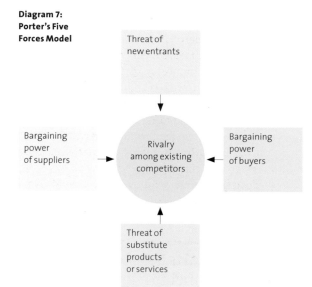

76

The business model

The business model of an organisation explains how the business idea, challenge and purpose of the organisation connect with the opportunities available in the external context, and what action will be taken that will benefit the organisation (for example, make a profit). The model directs strategy, that is, how the organisation will deliver on the purpose using its internal strengths and resources (i.e. its core competencies, capabilities and capacities). Strategies are then translated into a management action plan that details the business objectives, deliverables and key success factors.

'All design starts by leveraging the human instinct to relate, followed by translating the relationship into a tangible product or service, and then ideally adding a little surprise at the end to make the audience's effort worthwhile.'
John Maeda

The organisational context

Organisations are held together internally through a shared, common set of beliefs, values and ways of doing business that are defined in the vision and mission statement. The vision is the overall goal that all business activities are designed to help the organisation achieve (Ivanovic and Collin, 2005). Having a vision means that people are likely to be attracted to the organisation, its culture and its product and service offers; it also sets stakeholder expectations for what kind of behaviour and activities to anticipate. According to Wally Olins: 'the vision is the force that drives the organisation. It is what the organisation stands for, what it believes in' (Olins, 2008).

There are many new types of social enterprises, for example, that use 'commercial' business tools to achieve wider goals that are of benefit to society and the environment, or that take a long-term view of the ecological effects of their actions. Currently, many new enterprises are asking themselves 'what kind of business do we want to be?'

The management process

All organisational, decision-making processes are driven by strategy. Strategy should create sustainable competitive advantage – both through short-term, day-to-day planning, decision-making and delivering, and long-term vision about the right direction for the business to move in.

Strategy

Strategy describes the course of action and resources needed to achieve the vision of the organisation. It is 'a declaration of intent, defining where you want to be in the long term' (Bruce and Langdon, 2000). Strategy describes how the organisation plans on delivering on the mission and vision, and is translated into various business objectives, strategic plans and deliverables across different parts of the organisation.

The strategic direction of the organisation – how to move from where they currently are to a desired future position – is established by asking three key questions: (1) Where are we now? (2) Where do we want to go? (3) How do we get there? The essence of strategy, according to Michael Porter (1996), is choosing what not to do. 'Without trade-offs, there would be no need for choice and thus no need for strategy,' he claims.

Strategy operates at three levels in an organisation: *corporate strategy* sets the overall scope and direction of the organisation, and is aligned to the vision and mission; *business strategy* sets the goals and objectives for each of the specific business units (for example, a product or service line or division) or functional units (for example, marketing, finance and design). Finally, the *operational strategy* sets the action, execution and day-to-day operations and product/service delivery.

All levels of strategy set guidance for how managers are to add value to numerous organisational imperatives. The strategy dictates how different levels of the organisation develop their own corresponding objectives and strategies as relevant to their function, and how they choose to take action to implement the overall purpose and goals.

78

Diagram 8 demonstrates
how strategic management
involves understanding
the strategic position of an
organisation, its strategic
future choices, and how to
turn strategies into action.

Strategic positioning: the
impact on strategy of external
environment, internal
resources and competencies,
and the expectations of
stakeholders.

Strategic choices:
understanding the
underlying bases for future
strategy at both corporate
and business unit levels, and
the options for developing
strategy both in terms of the
directions in which strategy
might move and the methods
of development.

Strategy into action:
Organising for success,
building connections
between structures and
organisational processes
and emphasising the
importance of establishing
and maintaining internal and
external relationships and
boundaries.
*(Source: Johnson and
Scholes, 2006)*

Diagram 8:
The strategic management
of organisations

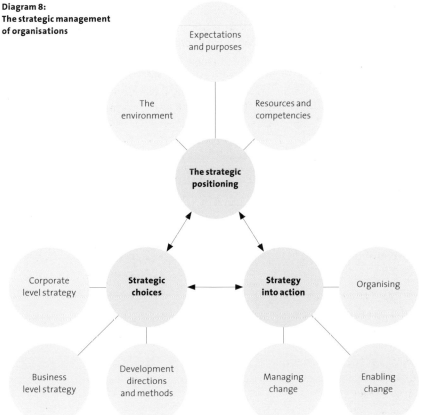

Core competencies and capabilities

All companies have assets (such as equipment and finances) and resources (such as processes and people) as well as certain things they are competent at, that they are capable of doing well. It is these 'competencies' and 'capabilities' that connect the 'value creation' activities of the company to a market of buyers, consumers and users, in order to make a profit.

According to Prahalad and Hamel (1990), a core competence is something an organisation does well. It provides benefit to the customer, it is hard for the competition to imitate, and it can be leveraged widely to many products and markets. They define a core capability (or capacity) as what you are good at, your 'knowledge base', what you have experience, know-how, expertise and skills for (Prahalad & Hamel 1990). Core competencies can lead to the creation of end products, but they can also be processes or steps in a supply chain as part of a number of businesses in a wider enterprise system.

Companies seek growth through their existing core competencies. According to John Kay (1995): 'corporate success is based on an effective match between the external relationships of the firm and its own distinctive capabilities.' The process of corporate strategy entails identifying the distinctive capabilities, selecting the best markets suited to these strengths, and building effective strategies to exploit them.

Companies may also seek new avenues for growth through 'value for money strategies' (increasing value whilst reducing costs), for example. In addition, if external market conditions change, companies may need to change their core business competencies in response. According to Likierman (2007): 'a successful, enduring business has to see itself as an "enterprise" and not a "fixed asset". It must adapt to survive.'

To survive, it may need to conduct an internal audit to identify hidden assets and competencies, leading to reorganisation, reinvention or repositioning of the organisation. Zook (2007) asserts that, typically, hidden assets may be discovered in: undervalued business platforms, untapped insights into consumers, and under-exploited capabilities.

1. Originating in London, UK, mOma believe that 'there's no such thing as a good day without a good morning.' Their purpose is to make available ready-to-eat, take-away breakfasts. mOma connect their products to people via stalls and outlets in busy commuter locations such as train stations. Their stands attract commuters who 'no longer have to skip breakfast'.

2. mOma research, test and trial new product lines in response to changing market conditions and consumer demands. Products such as their fruit jumble deliver satisfaction beyond the standard 'coffee and croissant' commuter breakfast.

3, 4, 5. Their products are healthy, filling, natural and delicious – what they describe as 'energy for people on the move'.

1

2

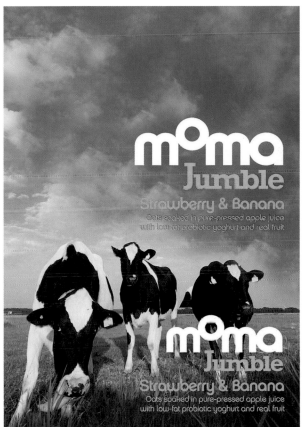

3

4

5

Business and enterprise planning

According to Peter Drucker (2005), 'the function of management is to produce results'. Producing results entails implementing the purpose, vision and strategy into all levels of the organisation – corporate, business and operational – and planning, co-ordinating, adapting and reviewing activities as appropriate to each level.

Business planning

Maintaining the day-to-day management of a business is as necessary as setting the direction for the growth of the business – in order to maintain sustainability for the long term.

Business planning is the framework for realising the potential of any business idea, whether a project or a whole enterprise. It is 'the art of choosing both where you want your business to go and how you think it will best get there' (Cohen, 1997), and sets down the structure for how the business opportunity will be realised through a set of organised activities. Business planning takes into account all internal business practices, and the 'analysis of processes, information systems, resources and team skills, to enable organisations to plan within their capabilities' (Bruce and Langdon, 2000). Activities are planned at the corporate level, the business unit level and the operational level, each with its own individually defined strategies, objectives and performance measures.

The corporate level deals with the setting of the strategic direction and how to create value from core competencies. The business level operates both independently within, and collaboratively across, functional (or business unit) areas to support corporate level strategies and build sustainable competitive advantage. Business units are set up to perform a specific function, aspect or specific enterprise-activity of the business – for example, marketing, human resources, sales, design, IT. The operational level involves the product, project, client teams or geographic regions, and is set up to support both the business strategy and the corporate strategy. Each level has associated objectives, goals and performance measures for success.

Traditionally, large organisations existed as fairly rigidly established organisational environments, with hierarchical structures and clearly defined, functionally separate business units (for example, Marketing, Finance, Operations, Engineering, Human Resources); and operational, project or programme divisions. These units had a set purpose, resources, accountability, targets, responsibilities and performance measures. In small enterprises, however, it is common that projects are carried out by networks of collaborators, whether individuals, teams or entities. Defined project or process teams will share a portfolio of responsibilities and deliverables in 'cross-functional' teams.

Diagram 9:
Three levels of strategy

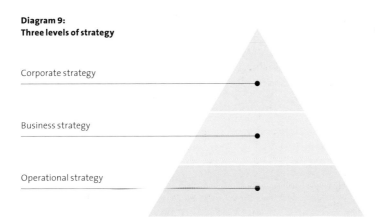

Corporate strategy

Business strategy

Operational strategy

The business plan

The business plan itself is a formal document and roadmap for initiating a new business idea or enterprise. It describes where you want the business to go, and forms an important part of any 'pitch' to secure resources, alliances, partners and stakeholder support to succeed. The purpose of a business plan is to define what you want the business to achieve – its objectives. It serves to focus a team, secure investment and funding and, if appropriate, a board of directors and shareholders. The plan is developed based on: identifying a gap in the market through market research; identifying what is needed to set up and operate the business (resource planning); identifying what processes and partnerships need to be in place, internally and externally, to deliver; and describing implementation and delivery.

The audience for the business plan should be carefully considered, since understanding the audience is crucial to selling the idea and securing support. The business case may be directed at an internal audience – for the launch of a new portfolio or product/service offer. Alternatively, it may be an external audience, in the case of an entirely new business or enterprise. Guy Kawasaki (2004) believes that: 'a good business plan is a detailed version of a pitch – as opposed to a pitch being a detailed version of a business plan.'

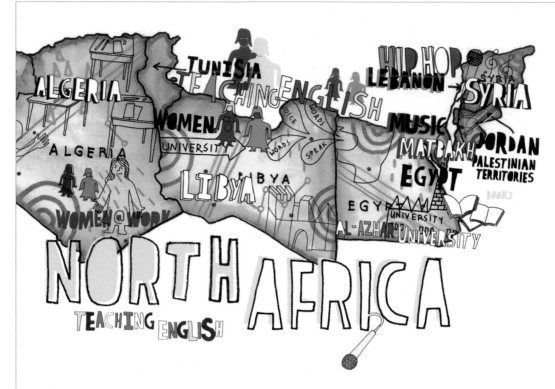

the centre of Cairo and started teaching English to 125 students from the Islamic Studies department. The project aims to produce graduates who not only excel in Islamic studies but are also able to communicate a moderate Islam around the world.

The Al-Azhar project also includes a quality assurance dimension, helping the university to achieve international benchmark standards in its teaching and curriculum design. This is resulting in a number of new UK university relationships, including an exchange programme between the University of Sheffield and the Department of Medicine for Women at Al-Azhar and an exchange of Al-Azhar deans with British academic institutions, focusing on quality assurance.

Al-Azhar is keen to develop the current project with us to engage other Islamic studies centres across the region. In doing so we would be creating new opportunities for thousands of students in the region, improving the quality of education and increasing intercultural understanding around the world.

Income trends
Measured in millions

8.6	13.8	2007–08
7.2	13.3	2006–07
6.1	12.9	2005–06
5.0	12.6	2004–05

■ Grant income
■ Other income

The region has received a significant increase in grant in line with corporate priorities. This will further increase in 2008–09. Overall, income has grown owing to an increase in English teaching across the region and an increase in client-funded project work in Libya.

Country share of income
Measured in millions
Country in **bold** denotes head office

FCO GRANT

OTHER INCOME

	FCO GRANT	OTHER INCOME	TOTAL
● EGYPT	2.0	5.0	7.0
● **JORDAN**	1.0	2.3	3.3
● LEBANON	0.6	0.5	1.1
● LIBYA	0.6	1.6	2.2
● MOROCCO	0.9	1.3	2.2
● PALESTINIAN TERRITORIES	1.6	0.1	1.7
● SYRIA	0.9	2.0	2.9
● TUNISIA AND ALGERIA	0.7	1.0	1.7
● REGIONAL BUDGET	0.4	0.0	0.4
TOTAL	8.6	13.8	22.4

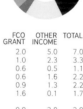

2. The British Council is the UK's international organisation for educational opportunities and cultural relations. As an organisation, they have offices in over 100 countries, which are sub-divided into 11 regions. Their Annual Report (facing page) designed by Navig8, communicates each region's individual strategies, priorities and aspirations, which, nonetheless, are still consistent with the overall vision, purpose and mission of the British Council – that of building cultural relations.

Table 5: A typical business plan structure

Title	The core idea or brand
Introduction	Company contact details, executive summary
Description of the company (if existing company)	Nature of the business, main activities, background, organisational structure, key people (both individuals and outside collaborators/suppliers)
The business problem	The context and the opportunity available
The business solution	What it is, how it will be achieved (the strategy), target audience
The business model	How the purpose and opportunity connect, profitably
The USP of the offer	What makes the offer different
The competition	Who else is competing within your industry, or for your customers
Marketing and sales plan	How to connect to audiences, users and consumers, how to launch the offer
Financial plan	Growth projections, summary of profits, forecasts and ROI (as relevant)
Funding requirements	Funds needed, sources of funding
Risk	Potential problems and rewards
Current status	Next steps
Appendices	Funding plan (P & L account, balance sheet, cash flow forecasts, assets, working capital) Costing plan (sales forecast, cost of sales forecast, margins) Overhead plan (associated costs)

Source: adapted from Cohen (1997) and Kawasaki (2004)

Management practice

Delivering on visions, goals and objectives requires the co-ordination and commitment of resources, processes and people, both horizontally and vertically, throughout an organisation. The roles and responsibilities of individuals and teams, and the motivations, incentives and reward mechanisms involved, define the overall culture and behaviour of the organisation. Since design managers are typically used to working across organisational departments and have a good understanding of product and service design and customer delivery, they are well placed to identify additional opportunities for adding value outside of traditional departmental objectives.

Organisational culture and behaviour

All companies have internal structures and frameworks in place to manage the processes of the enterprise, and to get goods and services to the market, to customers and end-users. But how motivated and committed employees are to delivering on the organisational purpose depends significantly on the culture of the organisation, so that the culture supports the strategic objectives. Aligning individual and organisational incentives and behaviour typically leads to a strong sense of belonging to, and delivering on, a common vision and values. It also encourages a culture that enables employees to add value at all levels.

Peter Drucker's management approach was most concerned with how managers could make the most of human resources, especially with regard to productivity and profitability. His five key principles of management involve: first, setting objectives; secondly, organising; thirdly, motivating and communicating; fourthly, establishing measures of performance; and finally, developing people, including the self, as Hutton and Holbeche summarise (2007).

Diagram 10:
Auditing organisational
culture and behaviour

| Mission | Guides our | Objectives | Achieved by fulfilling | Critical success factors | Measured using | Key performance indicators |

Organisational systems and processes

Corporate level strategy drives business level strategy, which in turn dictates the operational level strategy – through objectives, goals, critical success factors (CSF) and key performance indicators (KPI). According to Clark (2008), critical success factors (the factors critical to success), and key performance indicators (the measures of successful performance), have a great influence on organisational behaviour, since rewards generally motivate behaviour. These measures define the incentives for people to succeed in an organisation.

Linking the vision, mission, objectives, critical success factors and key performance indicators helps organisations know where they are going (mission statement and purpose), what needs to be done (objectives and goals), and what actions and results define success (success factors and performance indicators) – all of which are intended to add value directly to the organisation, and indirectly to the customer (Clark, 2008). Objectives are quantifiable, specific, measurable, attainable, relevant and time-bound. Goals, conversely, can be qualifiable and are therefore more open-ended.

Diagram 10. How well is an organisation doing? One way that design managers can support business objectives is to look at ways to bring fresh thinking to the organisation in terms of how to fulfil the mission, objectives, critical success factors and key performance indicators (facing page). (*Source: Clark, 2008*)

Diagram 11. Habits are internalised principles and patterns of behaviour that can help – or hinder – individual and organisational success. Covey's *Seven Habits* (below) address the development of personal growth from dependence (directed, nurtured, sustained), to interdependence (self-reliant, capable, self-mastery), to interdependence (teamwork, cooperation, communication). (*Source: adapted from Covey, 1990*)

**Diagram 11:
Auditing organisational systems and processes**

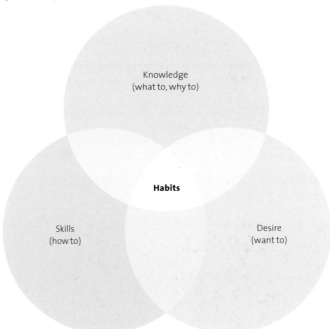

Knowledge (what to, why to)

Skills (how to)

Habits

Desire (want to)

Interpersonal relations

All enterprises need clear, solid management processes, as well as people with the knowledge and skills required to manage and organise the business efficiently and effectively. In order to identify and exploit business and creative opportunities and relationships in the wider context, it is necessary to operate both independently and within wider collaborative networks of small and large organisations. Generating commitment to, and delivering results for a project, is more likely to succeed when teams of people work well together to achieve end results, and are motivated to pursue set targets and objectives.

Within organisations, people are expected to work well individually as well as in teams. The key skills (or competencies) of good design managers – and qualities that all organisations can develop in their employees – are: time-keeping, presentation skills, communication skills (written and spoken), delegating, leadership and management skills, teamworking, motivating, managing relationships, stakeholder and management buy-in, negotiating personnel management and conflict resolution.

People with 'emotional intelligence' – the ability to understand their own personal feelings and those of other people, to take other people's feelings into account when reacting to decisions and to respond to people's feelings in a thoughtful way, are more likely to work well in teams (Goleman, 1995). Goleman identified the five 'domains' of emotional intelligence: first, knowing your emotions; secondly, managing your own emotions; thirdly, motivating yourself; fourthly, recognising and understanding other people's emotions; and finally, managing relationships, that is, managing the emotions of others.

Table 6: Ten steps to effective team working

Step 1: focus the team	Step 6: review team performance
Get acquainted	Complete evaluation
Write the team charter	Discuss
Begin documentation	Decide actions

Step 2: assign roles	Step 7: complete the work
Review team functions	Aim for completion
Assign roles	Overcome problems
Clarify responsibilities	Document results

Step 3: establish guidelines	Step 8: publish the results
Review healthy team behaviours	Set communication goals
Decide team guidelines	Plan the communication
Add a team charter	Present/publish

Step 4: plan the work	Step 9: reward the team
Lay out major goals	Celebrate milestones as a team
Break into tasks	Recognise the team in the organisation
Schedule tasks	

Step 5: do the work	Step 10: move on
Meet regularly	Disband
Update action items	Restructure, or
Communicate	Renew
Address problems	

Source: Rees, 1997

Table 6. Effective teamworking falls into three phases: getting organised, producing the results, and closing the project. Teams need clear goals, and the ability to be led or to collaborate to reach consensus. Resources and support must be available; and co-ordination and communication needs to be guided, typically by a project or design manager. Table 6 shows the appropriate steps that can be taken to ensure good teamwork.

89

Business administration

Good administrative systems and processes enable effective day-to-day management. Design managers who can understand the ways in which a business is managed are also in a position to help identify opportunities for design.

Outsourcing

Companies outsource tasks for which they do not have an in-house competency, or that can be completed out of house more effectively, efficiently and expertly. It allows them to focus on their core competencies and activities. Outsourcing can reduce and improve cost structures, overheads, and enable more competitive pricing. It will also strengthen a competitive position, for example, by improving the way that products and services are delivered to customers. Freelance and contract staff are frequently used on design projects, as they are a flexible and more cost-effective way to commit professional design skills to short-term projects

Invoices and purchase orders

In order to procure goods and services from suppliers, client organisations usually raise a purchase order with a description of what is required. Suppliers, in return, raise invoices in order to be paid. Both include information about: the order number, the company and person placing the order, what is being ordered and its value, VAT if applicable, the terms of payment (for example, 60 days), and the rate of interest charged if the bill is not settled in time.

If the company is VAT registered, then legally the company's name, address, registered number and place of registration must be stated on the invoice.

Contracts

A contract is a formal and legally enforceable indication that two parties want to work together. For a contract to exist, an offer needs to be made, and an acceptance secured. The acceptance can be written, verbal or implied by conduct. It is, of course, advisable to confirm all contracts in writing, to minimise disagreements and disputes. Some common contracts in the design industry are: NDAs (non-disclosure agreements) and other contracts that protect ideas; IP (intellectual property) protection; employment engagement and termination; and procurement of goods and services.

Credit and debt

Businesses need to proactively manage credit and debt, whether dealing with banks, suppliers, or governmental income tax issues. When applying for credit, a process of 'credit scoring' enables 'credit-worthiness' to be established, so influencing what credit terms will be offered. Credit reference agencies look at credit history to assess the risk of lending. Typically, credit incurs interest – called an APR or annual percent rate – chargeable as a penalty if payment dates are missed or credit limits exceeded. In the event of debt, try to agree manageable payment terms with creditors, look at ways to consolidate debts and seek advice – before bankruptcy or insolvency.

90

1. The statement of financial activities for the British Council. In order to comply with governmental administrative regulations, an independent auditor from a source outside of the British Council must review and confirm that the financial statements have been prepared under the accounting policies set out within the annual report, and that they comply with HM Treasury guidance.

2. The British Council's internal control system is designed to manage risk to a reasonable level rather than to eliminate all risk of failure. It is based on a continuing process designed to identify and prioritise the risks to the achievement of policies, aims and objectives, to evaluate the likelihood of those risks being realised and the impact likely should they be realised, and to manage them efficiently, effectively and economically.

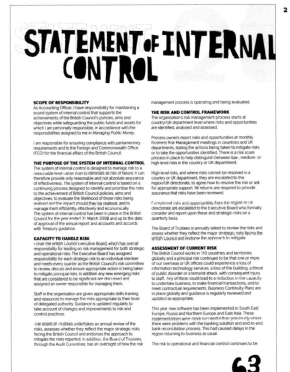

Risk management

Risk awareness and the ability to identify, evaluate and manage risk is a key part of effective management thinking. Individual people, and whole organisational cultures, have different levels of comfort in risk-taking, risk-acceptance and risk-aversion. When commencing a new project, it is worth establishing – not assuming – how much risk an organisation is prepared to take.

For clients, design agencies and suppliers, starting a new working relationship is always a risk, so taking the time to establish trust and good communication is time well invested, as it tends to result in long-term liaisons. When commencing relationships with new suppliers, large organisations usually perform a 'risk analysis' on potential clients or suppliers, with the aim of reducing their exposure to financial or reputation risk. Managers responsible for procuring goods and services take a view on the risk involved, and make decisions on accepting, reducing or rejecting the risk.

Business success

Just as there are different ways to create value, there are different ways to measure value. What does success look like? How do you measure corporate success? How do we evaluate success in business? What business performance measures are most applicable in management processes, and crucially, important to design?

Value

According to John Kay (1995), 'the achievement of any company is measured by its ability to add value – to create an output which is worth more than the costs of the input which it uses.' What we value, however, can differ according to our cultural and regional locations; in the United States, for example, the focus is typically on measuring profit, whereas in Europe, the focus tends rather to be on improving quality of life.

Performance measurement

Key performance indicators (KPIs) are used by businesses to achieve critical success factors, and typically inform organisations about how well they are doing. Performance, however, is about how well a task is performed, not whether an actual activity has been completed or not. KPIs need to be SMART; Specific, Measurable, Achievable, Realistic and Timed. As with all management information, KPIs must be justified in terms of costs and benefits.

Measures of success can include both quantitative (numerical) and qualitative measures, such as size, market share, profitability, shareholder value, (technical) efficiency, reputation and, increasingly, innovation capability. It is good practice to monitor performance in business processes and gain feedback to continually develop improved goods and service offerings – as well as inform organisational learning, reinvestment of capital and re-evaluation of success criteria. What new measures could be used that more appropriately reflect and celebrate the success achieved?

Protecting the business value of design

When legally registered, protected and exploited, creative or intangible assets within an organisation – intellectual property assets such as names, images, concepts, designs, music and writing – can be exploited to generate additional revenue streams and increase the value of how design is perceived within the organisation. For example, by registering and protecting an idea for an innovative new product or service, other companies wanting to offer the same product or service will have to enter a licensing agreement or royalty arrangement, or will have to buy the rights. Protecting creative and intellectual assets is a valuable form of competitive advantage as other companies will be prohibited from copying, manufacturing or otherwise 'ripping off' the offer. Intellectual property can be registered in the form of trademarks, copyrights, patents, licensing agreements, design rights and transfer of ownership.

1, 2, 3. The British Council's annual report illustrates one way to measure business performance. After setting up programmes and geographical priorities, they use a score card to measure business performance in: the impact they make; the audiences they engage with and reach; and the level of satisfaction of their customers and stakeholders. These factors are measured through six corporate outputs (below). They measure year-on-year results, as well as progress against established baselines, trends, and improving future levels of performance (bottom).

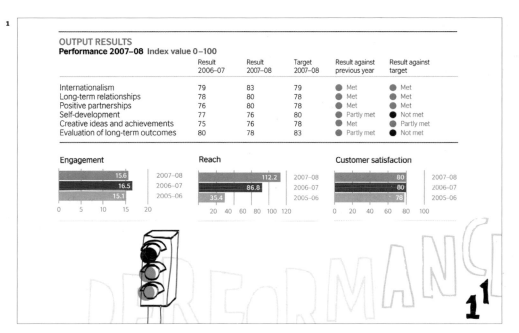

OUTPUT RESULTS
Performance 2007–08 Index value 0–100

	Result 2006–07	Result 2007–08	Target 2007–08	Result against previous year	Result against target
Internationalism	79	83	79	● Met	● Met
Long-term relationships	78	80	78	● Met	● Met
Positive partnerships	76	80	78	● Met	● Met
Self-development	77	76	80	● Partly met	● Not met
Creative ideas and achievements	75	76	78	● Met	● Partly met
Evaluation of long-term outcomes	80	78	83	● Partly met	● Not met

Engagement

15.6	2007–08
16.5	2006–07
15.1	2005–06

0 5 10 15 20

Reach

112.2	2007–08
86.8	2006–07
35.4	2005–06

20 40 60 80 100 120

Customer satisfaction

80	2007–08
80	2006–07
78	2005–06

0 20 40 60 80 100

CORPORATE PERFORMANCE

INDICATOR
● Not met
● Partly met
● Met

Impact perspective corporate outputs	RESULT 2006–07	RESULT 2007–08	TARGET 2007–08	RESULT AGAINST PREVIOUS YEAR	RESULT AGAINST TARGET
Internationalism Relationships brokered by the British Council broaden the international view of young people	79	83	79	●	●
Long-term relationships An increase in the number of quality relationships between the UK and other countries*	78	80	78	●	●
Positive partnerships The UK is increasingly recognised as a country of choice for partnering social change	76	80	78	●	●
Self-development The UK is increasingly recognised as a country able to satisfy aspirations for self-development	77	76	80	●	●
Creative ideas and achievements The UK is increasingly recognised for its creative ideas and achievements	75	76	78	●	●
ELTO (Evaluation of long-term outcomes) Evidence from senior decisions-makers and influencers – T1 and T2*	80	78	83	●	●
Strengthening of ties with the UK resulting from new or continuing engagement with the British Council	74	68	78	●	●
Personal/organisational beneficial changes resulting from new or continuing engagement with the British Council	83	82	88	●	●

*We use the following definitions for our target audiences:
T1 High-level decision-maker; T2 Influencer or leading professional; T3 People with potential.

51

CORPORATE PERFORMANCE (CONTINUED)

INDICATOR
● Not met
● Partly met
● Met

Reputation and satisfaction perspective	RESULT 2006–07	RESULT 2007–08	TARGET 2007–08	RESULT AGAINST PREVIOUS YEAR	RESULT AGAINST TARGET
Customers satisfied with the British Council	80	80	82	●	●
Customers perceive the British Council as innovative	83	87	82	●	●
Foreign and Commonwealth Office satisfied with the British Council*	87	76	87	●	●

Audience perspective	RESULT 2006–07	RESULT 2007–08	RESULT AGAINST PREVIOUS YEAR
Engaged through British Council projects, programmes and services*			
Remote reach (millions)	86.8 million	112.2 million	●
Engagement (millions)	16.5 million	15.6 million	●
A high proportion of T1 (high-level decision-makers and leaders) significantly engaged with the British Council	9,063	13,353	●
More international students in UK higher education	HE 356,080 (2005–06 results)	HE 376,190 (2006–07 results)	●
More international students in UK further education	FE 87,173 (2005–06 results)	FE 84,340 (2006–07 results)	●
Increasing numbers of participants pursuing British Council offered opportunities for self-development			
Numbers of teaching centre students and examinations candidates (millions)	1.4 million	1.5 million	●
Increasing numbers of young people involved in links leading to broader international views (millions)	7.5 million	8 million	●

*The results from the Heads of Mission survey for 2007–08 are not strictly comparable with those for 2006–07 owing to differences in the survey coverage and data collection methodology

52

MAS Holdings: enterprising ethical retailing

94

case study

Organisations that connect how they are managed with the needs of the local community in which they are based are in a strong position to bring their vision and values to life, in a way that makes a real difference to both society and business. With a turnover of US $700 million, MAS Holdings is South Asia's largest intimate apparel manufacturer, and the region's most rapidly growing provider of competition sportswear. Their global operations include design studios and 28 world-class manufacturing facilities made up of an international team of over 45,000 people.

As well as being an operationally successful business, MAS Holdings are committed to ethical and sustainable practices and are committed to positioning Sri Lanka as the number one destination for ethical clothing. The value chain of their global operations incorporates a seamless concept-to-delivery solution, including an award-winning amalgamation of research and innovation, design and development, manufacturing excellence and raw material supply. Their SBUs (Strategic Business Units) are WRAP certified (that is, adhering to the criteria of Worldwide Responsible Apparel Production), carrying the only A grades in the region. According to Holcim, apparel production and export accounts for two-thirds of Sri Lanka's industry (Holcim, 2008).

MAS divisions

Brothers Mahesh, Ajay and Sharad Amalean set up MAS Holdings in 1987. MAS Intimates (as a division specialising in underwear) sprang up later in 2005. It is the largest division, with an annual turnover of US $260 million, and is a 'strategic vendor' for Nike, Marks & Spencer and Victoria's Secret. They work together to tackle common challenges, such as equal opportunities and supporting local communities. Social concerns influenced their decision to build factories in rural areas near their potential workforce, with the beneficial aim of putting money back into local communities and creating better-trained, happier and more loyal employees who could live and work close to their homes.

MAS Active is the fastest-growing provider of competition sportswear and fashion leisurewear in the region, supplying their joint venture partner, Speedo, their strategic business partner, Nike, and other leading brands such as Adidas and Columbia. They opened the first dedicated swimwear plant in Sri Lanka, from where they produce competition swimwear for the Olympics. In addition, they provide national and international sports personalities with performance-enhancing attire – including clothing for the 'world champion' Sri Lankan cricket team.

1. Design and innovation are the keys to MAS's competitive edge. Having built strong value chain partnerships, MAS work closely with customers, offering support throughout the production process, from concept to manufacturing (<www.masholdings.com>). MAS are a strategic partner for NIKE, acting as a supplier of their competition sportswear, MAS Active (left).

2. MAS Eco-Go Beyond aims to improve lives as one of the many programmes and initiatives that fall under their CSR framework. MAS Eco-Go Beyond refers to a programme that teaches sustainability to community schoolchildren, thereby supporting community, organisation, sports and environment. This framework supports community education, infrastructure and sustainable livelihoods; helps people realise their potential; and builds the sense of a cohesive family (www.masholdings. com). Pictured (left) is a specific project focused on educating schoolchildren on sustainability, an example of one programme that exists within MAS's CSR framework.

3. MAS 'Women Go Beyond' Programme: as part of this initiative, the computer centre at MAS's Slimline factory conducts free, six-month IT training courses for machine operators and their families.

3

4

4. Corporate Social Responsibility (CSR) lies at the heart of MAS, and living their ethical policies is an important part of their organisational vision and reporting systems. The focus on creating healthy working environments near the rural areas where many employees actually live, for example, ensures MAS's reputation and credentials in CSR, and helps differentiate them from many of their competitors. This image shows recent coverage of MAS and its ethical policies in *World Business* magazine.

Organisational culture

With a culture of progressive management, MAS as an organisation 'seeks to empower people at all levels'. They seek to continually 'raise the bar on accepted standards of ethics and best practices in global industry' – and this is demonstrated not only through economic success, but through high levels of environmental and social performance. 'Guaranteeing employee well-being, while considering their rights and means of empowerment, is central to our people-philosophy. Our working practices, including lean operating systems and processes, give our employees authority, from the sewing line, up' (<www.masholdings.com>).

The speed of product development processes helps them both to set the benchmark for the competition and to realise competitive advantage.

MAS responsibility

To MAS, corporate responsibility (CR) is about 'doing the right thing'. Social sustainability has been embedded in the company DNA from the beginning, and enables them to partner with customers on key CR initiatives as a 'responsible corporate' – as well as setting the context for MAS to localise their operations and become a part of the communities in which they are based.

Their key CR initiatives are: MAS Women Go Beyond (championing women's empowerment in the global apparel industry); and MAS Eco Go Beyond (educating the next generation on sustainability).

Strategic partnerships

MAS actively seek strategic partnerships which are mutually productive and profitable. They consider design and innovation to be key to their competitive edge; through how they strengthen their value chain partnerships, to how they collaborate with customers and support the design and development process, from concept to production. The Active design and development team creates 'powerful value chain partnerships with regional presence, supply chain integration and highly co-ordinated and synchronised process controls' (<www.masholdings.com>).

case study

MAS Intimates Thurulie

As an example of their commitment to sustainability, MAS developed an 'eco-venture' – MAS Intimates Thurulie – the first eco-manufacturing plant for apparel, one powered solely by carbon-neutral sources.

Designed around the principles of lean manufacturing, the factory is profitable to operate (in terms of energy efficiency, operational efficiency and productivity), has revived an historic industrial centre by re-establishing a local economic base, and provides long-term employment for 1300 local people (Holcim, 2008). Instead of one large factory hall, lean-production standards are used – ones that offer smaller production areas with discrete value streams – from cutting fabric to packaging finished garments. To enhance equality and direct collaboration, production areas and offices are visually connected, with no obstructive columns in the way. Strict selection criteria were used when specifying building materials for the design, inspired by Sri Lankan architecture.

All these actions help to stimulate long-term stability, health and well-being both in the region – socially, economically and environmentally – and also in the people themselves. The building, its work environment and the preservation of the natural habitat of the surroundings provide staff with high levels of beauty, comfort, respect and dignity; additional services such as buses, free lunches, medical care and banking facilities are also available on site. This follows the belief that 'towns and buildings must respond to emotional and psychological needs by providing stimulating environments, raising awareness of important values, inspiring the human spirit, and bonding society' (Holcim, 2008).

The Holcim Foundation for Sustainable Construction developed five 'target issues' to help measure how the building contributes to sustainable development: balanced environmental, social and economic performance; the creation of good neighbourhoods, towns and cities; and the need for significant advancements that can be applied on a broad scale. Both MAS Holdings and Marks & Spencer have succeeded in presenting the plant as 'an iconic model for green manufacturing, one which sets new standards for design, construction and operation' (Holcim, 2008).

5

6

5, 6. As a building, MAS Intimates Thurulie is 'a visionary departure from the traditional factory, setting new standards for ethics and environmental stewardship in manufacturing' (Holcim, 2008). It is a state of the art flagship factory for MAS Holdings, a 'model building' for Marks & Spencer's Plan A eco-initiative, and a globally publicised icon symbolising the beliefs and values of MAS.

Ruedi Alexander Müller-Beyeler
TATIN Scoping Complexity

TATIN Scoping Complexity is an international company of specialists in designing for change and innovation.

Management skills: complexity, change and innovation

'Car manufacturers can build cars really well. They are car developers with heart and soul. Therefore, they probably still think of cars when they reflect on alternative means of locomotion; leading to ideas about alternative car concepts but probably not to revolutionary new ideas, such as using the Internet as a travel vehicle. The notion that people could travel on the net instead of driving cars can be threatening to car manufacturers, because everything they know and can do well would necessarily be questioned.

'The status of car manufacturing at the beginning of the 21st century is an example of how companies – even very big organisations – are built for specific purposes. Know-how and competence have been developed, structures have been designed as a result, and the culture has been optimised accordingly. A change from the inside or the outside irritates such a system.

'To be able to understand and estimate to what extent innovation and change are possible in a company, as a design manager, I must first understand exactly what an organisation stands for. What does it do well? How does it think and act? What is its business model? Does the new strategy under consideration actually fit? I need to understand what a car manufacturer means – and does not mean – when talking of mobility.

'Because companies are built for specific products, services and procedures and they have been successful with these in the past, as design manager I must examine the robustness of a new strategy as presented to me by the board of directors. Robust means compatible with the competencies of the company, for example, in the context of competence, structure and culture. Is the company really willing and able to develop and implement something new?

'Is it ready to bear the consequences and to question what has been successful until now? Or does it want to follow what other companies are doing and thereby not change at all? Does the car company want to make people mobile or simply build a new car that uses less fuel?

contextual perspectives

'Real or disruptive innovation can change the world and thereby probably changes the company itself. Therefore, the company must develop new capabilities, build up new structures and change its culture. As a design manager, I must ask if the company is ready to change when the strategy demands innovation, and I must be aware that I am always a bit of a change manager in the company too. This means that design processes are simultaneously also change processes. Design management can influence the company in the long term and help to create a breakthrough if I apply methods which facilitate working towards a goal and at the same time thereby enable, support and embed change in the company.

'My goal as a design manager is to develop the design process so that transformation can be recognised and accepted as an opportunity by the organisation. In this way, design management will provide the company with a double benefit.

'First, the design process will lead to a result, for example, a new product, a new service or a new business model; secondly, the design process can enable structural, cultural and procedural transformation within the company, thereby opening space for future development. Then, the result is perhaps not only a car that uses less fuel, but also a company full of enthusiasm, inspired to think further into the future.'

Ruedi Alexander Müller-Beyeler
Tatin Scoping Complexity, Switzerland

'Real or disruptive innovation can change the world and thereby probably changes the company itself.'

101

Kevin McCullagh
Plan

Plan is a product strategy consultancy. It helps companies work out what to do next by bringing more clarity to the front end of product planning.

Business and enterprise

'Design managers had a good 10 years between 1997 and 2007. The challenges in the good times were the result of positive developments such as design's elevation up the management agenda, the expansion of its remit, and the resulting complexity that came with more responsibility and exposure. A harsher business climate will lead to a different set of demands.

'In hindsight, two events in 1997 set the scene for design's rise. In the UK, Tony Blair's New Labour was elected with a mandate to modernise Britain, and quickly elevated its creative industries to the forefront of economic policy – a strategy that would be replicated around the world in the form of countless creative sector policies. Creativity and innovation were set to become buzzwords amongst political and business leaders.

'In the same year, Steve Jobs returned to Apple, which soon became the totemic case study of how to out-innovate the competition through smart design. As a design strategy consultant in this period, I lost count of how many brand directors' strategy amounted to little more than aspiring to be the "Apple of our category". The days of putting the case for the importance of design were replaced by fighting off calls from different parts of the business wanting to join the design party.

'"Design thinking", the hazily defined notion that designers are well equipped to tackle a wide range of business problems, can be seen as a high-water mark of this euphoria.

'A critique began to surface in 2007, with questions raised about design's sustainability credentials and its obsession with superficial novelty. *Business Week* magazine also reported an "innovation backlash" in the same year. The recession has only served to sharpen the questions for design managers.

'The idea of design as a silver bullet has lost currency. As one design manager put it to me recently, "even turkeys can fly in a tornado"; but when the tailwind dropped, many design managers were left gliding. Greater exposure to senior management had left many... well... exposed.

'The concern is that too much time has been spent trying to outsmart the MBAs, and that design managers have lost their focus on delivering great design. The most common response to this feeling of corporate over-stretch, is to regroup and go back-to-basics, with many managers pining to just roll up their sleeves and get down to designing.

'While this reaction to a sense of mission creep is understandable, it risks jettisoning some important gains. It is vital that design does not become viewed as part of the froth of the go-go years. While design is not a replacement for business strategy, it also has more to offer than experience aesthetics. One of the big challenges in the next period will be to define the boundaries of what design departments can and can't usefully contribute to with more rigour and precision.

'Design and innovation have undoubtedly become emptied of much of their meaning through over-use (and abuse), but we should also resist the flight to new buzzwords. There is no alternative to explaining – in longhand – how design can contribute to business success as specifically as we can. We should also not shy away from explaining how difficult it is to deliver great design; and that while there is a design process it is not a general-purpose methodology, but a specialist one that must be executed by experienced and talented designers.'

Kevin McCullagh
Director, Plan, UK

'Design and innovation have undoubtedly become emptied of much of their meaning through over-use (and abuse), but we should also resist the flight to new buzzwords. There is no alternative to explaining – in longhand – how design can contribute to business success as specifically as we can.'

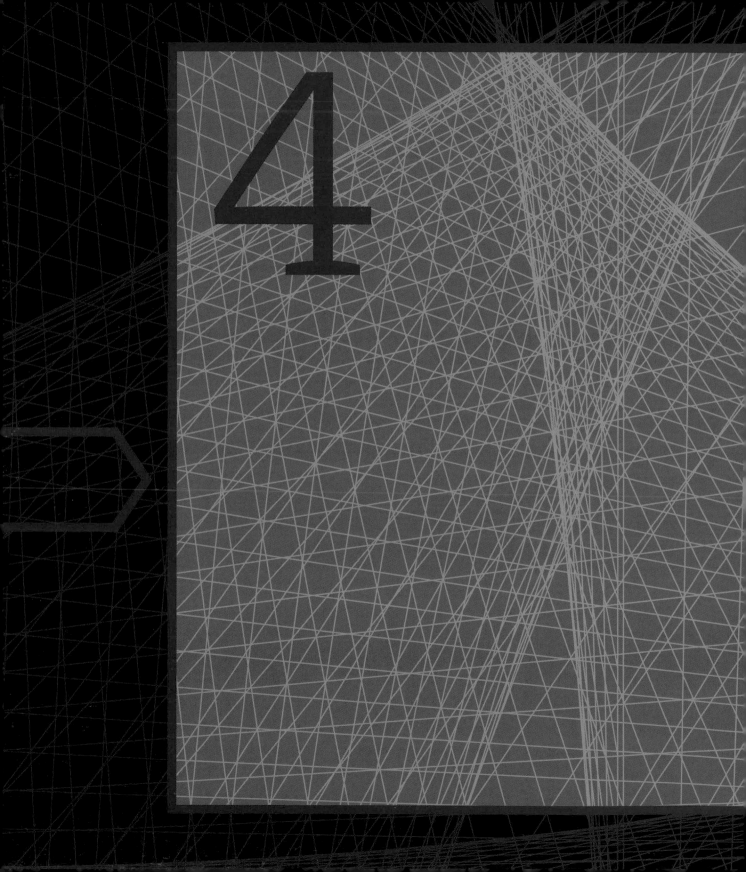

Accounting and finance

The financial organisation

The world of finance is unclear to most designers, yet engaging in conversations about finance and managing money effectively are important parts of ensuring the survival of any type of business. Knowing the basics of financial management, how performance is reported, and how design is valued therein, will help designers 'understand the numbers', and be aware of how financial information is used in decision-making processes.

Finance and accounting

Finance is the life blood of any company or business, and without it organisations would perish. Finance concerns the management of money: how money is raised, utilised and spent by an individual or company. Those with expertise in finance can instantly comprehend the state of a business by analysing financial figures and measures. They are also able to use planning, budgetary and forecasting tools to effectively manage current and future organisational requirements. The way in which the numbers are presented and controlled depends on the structure and scale of the particular company.

Most large organisations have a finance department with associated accounting procedures, whereas smaller companies may have one person responsible for all accounting and financial management decisions.

Sole practitioners tend to outsource their finances to an external accountant. Despite the less than glamorous stereotypical image of accountants, the influence that they have on the commercial aspects and ultimately success of a business is profound. Accounting is 'the work of recording money paid, received, borrowed or owed' (Ivanovic and Collin, *2005*).

Financial processes

Financial accounting: records monetary transactions (for example, book-keeping), and its audience is generally external. Management accounting focuses on the creation of value for stakeholders (for example, ensuring the efficient use of resources) and it is used primarily by management.

Financial reporting: shows how a company is performing. It is the process used to explain the company's strategy to investors and markets, and record and communicate their current financial position in terms of assets and debts. The financial reporting cycle takes place at defined intervals (usually annually). Within the financial reporting process there are statutory reporting requirements, to demonstrate regulatory compliance (for legal, government, and tax purposes), and management reporting requirements, to present the financial value, performance and integrity of the company (for analysts, investors and auditors).

1. Based in the United Kingdom, Nottingham Community Housing Association (NCHA) have traditional values of service with an innovative approach. Purple Circle reflected this in the design approach to their 2008 annual report. Tradition is reflected in the retrospective style of both words and pictures, with the design linking back to NCHA's origins in the early 1970s

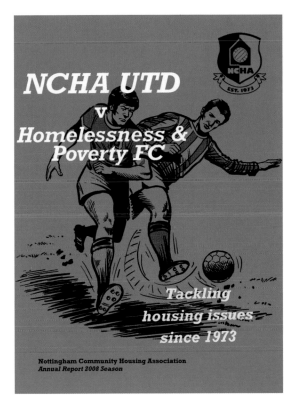

Organisational goals

Most finance directors work with a board to achieve the strategic financial goals for the business whilst being fully responsible for the day-to-day running of the accounting and financial side of the company. Their skills in financial analysis are used across the business to support both internal decision-making processes and external reporting processes.

Ultimately, it is important to view the financial strategy in the context of the wider organisational strategic goals and objectives, and in relation to the customers themselves. Otherwise, making short-term profit 'for profit's sake' would be the goal, which may undermine the long-term financial stability and sustainability of the organisation.

Design managers need to balance commercial and creative objectives. In order to create, grow and exploit opportunities available to design, they may need to question the status quo of how figures are used to make decisions. Having even a basic knowledge of finance can help design managers helpfully support and exert influence within the context of a management team.

Does the way in which success is defined and measured need to be challenged, so as to reflect favourably on design? Are there opportunities to introduce new, design-beneficial ways to measure value and success ?

Financial accounting

All companies are required to keep accounts that record their financial status and report on their financial dealings. This is performed using a set of financial statements.

Financial statements

Balance sheet: A balance sheet shows the state of a company at a certain date. It states the current financial balance of the company at that point in time, in terms of assets (land, buildings, stock, cash, money owed, prepaid expenses) and liabilities (what it owes – accounts payable, loans, provisions for future expenses). The net of these, that is, assets less liabilities, will equal the owners or shareholders' equity (that is, the net assets that are spread amongst the shareholders of the business).

More specifically, assets are said to be either fixed assets (the present value of inventory, equipment, buildings, vehicles), or current assets (stock, debtors, money in the bank and cash). The essential difference is that current assets are able to be more easily and swiftly converted into cash. Current liabilities include bank loans and overdrafts, creditors and debts. Long-term loans are, for example, things like mortgages.

In general, the assets 'A' (such as inventory, equipment and buildings) are equal to the liabilities 'L' (such as bank loans, creditors or money owed to suppliers) plus the owners' equity, 'OE' (such as the owners' own money). This is expressed as $A = L + OE$.

Income statement: Also known as a 'profit and loss statement', the income statement describes the revenues, expenditure and subsequent profitability of the company over a defined period of time. It shows activity (expenses/cost of sales, and sales revenue) that has taken place since the last balance sheet. Tax is paid on the net profit.

The Income (I) is the difference between the revenue (R) generated, minus the expenses (E) incurred ($R - E = I$); if positive, the company is in profit, and if negative, the company made a loss during that period.

Cash flow statement: The cash flow statement records the flow of cash into and out of the company over a specific period of time (usually annually). Cash flow itself is a common cause of business failure; cash that comes into a company from sales needs to exceed expenditure, and situations such as delayed payment, reduced access to credit, increased financial cost or demands for early payment from suppliers can all affect cash flow.

Financial accounting: is the classification and recording of monetary transactions of an entity in accordance with established concepts, principles, accounting standards and legal requirements and their presentation, by means of income statements, balance sheets and cash-flow statements, during and at the end of an accounting period.

Management accounting: is the application of the principles of accounting and financial management to create, protect, preserve and increase value for the stakeholders of for-profit and not-for-profit enterprises in the public and private sectors.

Source: CIMA, 2005

Interpreting financial statements

Financial statements can help investors and creditors determine the past performance of the enterprise, predict future performance, and assess the capability of generating future cash flow. By analysing the movement of revenues, profits and deficits, and by being familiar with how the information is used within the decision-making (and the underlying assumptions and limitations of it), it is possible to assess the financial 'health' of an organisation. This will enable design managers to contribute insight and exert more influence.

Financial reporting

Financial reporting is the process by which companies disclose information concerning the financial activities of the business. These reports are used by investors and analysts to interpret the financial implications of the company's practices. The reports take the form of annual reports and annual accounts.

Annual reports and accounts

The annual report is used to communicate the past year's activities, to both the stakeholders and the wider general public. The chairman/CEO introduces the report with a summary of the year's activities, followed by a summary of the key financials, and a table of contents. Increasingly, information on environmental and social agendas is also included.

The annual accounts show the overall financial position of a company and includes financial statements; the balance sheet, statement of retained earnings, income statement, cash flow statement, notes to the financial statements and accounting policies. It can also be used to assess the sustainability of future cash flows.

In the UK the Accounting Standards Board (ASB) has identified eight criteria on operating and financial review reporting (OFR), which are considered to be the 'best practice' standard. These are: business overview; marketplace; strategy; key performance indicators; forward-looking information; risk management information; relationships; and responsibility (Radley Yeldar, 2008).

In large organisations, shareholders are invited to an annual general meeting (AGM), when they can question representatives from the company (directors, the board, the CEO) about its direction and management practices.

Corporate social responsibility (CSR) report

All businesses impact upon the economy, the environment and society, and business ethics are equally subject to an auditing process. CSR reports aim to balance economic growth with social and environmental sustainability. Their intent is to encourage sustainable business that balances short-term profitability with the creation of long-term economic 'goodwill'. CSRs evaluate the extent to which a company takes responsibility for its actions; and often includes measures of strategic and operational changes they implement, which leverage sustainability as a driver of performance.

Depending on the company, issues such as business ethics, social responsibility and corporate citizenship are included, and as such, they tend to be forward looking in their approach. How can we appropriately adapt our commercial business models to put sustainable growth and stakeholder needs at the core, build credible competitive advantage, and combine cost-saving initiatives while at the same time employing carbon-reducing and energy reduction strategies? The airline business of today is one example of an industry struggling to answer such questions.

1, 2, 3. The football analogy used by Purple Circle promotes the team ethic of Nottingham Community Housing Association (NCHA) and encourages people to read about their performance in their annual report and accounts (below and middle). The format has been made smaller to make it more portable and less expensive to print, and follows the football programme style. The board members are presented as a team (middle). The income statement and balance sheet (bottom) demonstrate the 'profit and loss' and 'financial balance' of the organisation respectively.

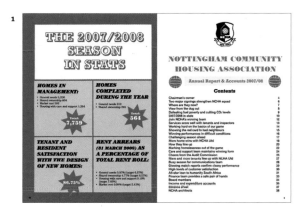

For many organisations, creating a separate CSR report is a way to embed sustainability into their annual report – and into their business models. Often, they are motivated by the opportunity to cut costs, improve productivity and increase revenue through initiatives such as improved energy efficiency programmes. Clearly, today's design managers will need to be aware of such new initiatives and be prepared to incorporate their principles into their plans.

Financial ratios

Financial ratios are used to quickly assess, amongst other things, profitability, activity, solvency and leverage, and the return to shareholders. They are used by investors for forecasting and valuation purposes – to try to predict future performance and growth in finances, and to comparatively evaluate a company's performance with other industry participants, so as to create a common basis from which to make assessments. There are some simple ratios that capture key elements of a company's performance. They are useful as a way to easily communicate where contributions are being made to organisational value.

Some examples include: return on investment (ROI), rate of return (ROR), return on sales (ROS), return on capital employed (ROCE), return on invested capital (ROIC), return on equity (ROE), sustainable growth rate (SGR), cost to income ratio and net profit margin.

113

Management accounting

Management accounting focuses on the reporting structures and control systems that can ensure that value of various kinds is created for stakeholders (that is, not just financial), and also that resources, capital and financial reporting structures are engaged as efficiently and effectively as possible. In terms of data, management accounting includes any information that is useful to the running of an organisation, whether in summary form or in detail.

Table 7: The nine functions of management accounting
Forming strategy
Planning
Determining capital structures and financing
Informing about operational decisions
Controlling operations and ensuring the efficient use of resources
Measuring and reporting on performance
Safeguarding assets
Implementing corporate governance procedures
Risk management and internal control

Source: CIMA, 2005

Capital investment

To run companies, and to undertake projects, money needs to be spent – on operational expenses and on capital investment. These are classified as 'expenditure', against which 'capital' may be secured and made available. We refer to 'assets' held by a company as capital. In the context of a company, capital investment involves making decisions to secure the company's long-term survival. Funds needed to run the company are typically secured in two ways: raising capital through 'equity' (by selling a share in the business or by injecting personal finances), or by raising money through 'debt', that is, by borrowing the money through, for example, a loan from a bank.

Cash outflows

It is important to understand and identify the costs it takes to run a business, make a product or provide a service, so that pricing strategies can be set and the company can make a profit – and not a loss. This involves collecting detailed financial data about products and services, and recording that data (Dyson, 2007).

Companies typically account for costs every month. Examples of data collected include instalments, which indicate something paid for over time, and depreciation, a cost-allocation procedure that recognises the decline in value of an asset in the expenses of an organisation, and shows up on an income statement as a cost. Appreciation, in contrast, would show as a profit.

Table 7. The Chartered Institute of Management Accountants (CIMA) in the UK identifies nine functions of management accounting, which it advises are to be included in financial reporting systems (facing page).

Table 8 demonstrates how balance sheets serve to balance assets (things we own), against liabilities (things we owe others). When operating a company, different types of costs need to be accounted for every month.

Table 9 provides an example of different ways that running costs can be classified for accounting purposes.

Table 8: The balance of capital assets

Classification costs	Direct (materials and labour) and indirect (expenses, consumables)
Revenue costs	For day-to-day running
Capital costs	For things that assist in running the business
Indirect/overhead costs	For example, administrative salaries, stationery
Behavioural costs	Variable costs (such as labour, materials) and fixed costs (such as lighting and heat)
Cost of goods sold (COGS)	Direct costs (fixed costs and variable costs)

Table 9: Ways to clarify running costs

	Definition	Examples
Capital assets	Fixed assets, for use over one year (i.e. long term)	Buildings, offices, factories, vehicles, equipment, computers, furniture
Capital liabilities	Fixed assets, over the long term	Long-term loans, mortgages, shares
Current assets	Current 'short-term' working capital (i.e. current assets less current liabilities)	Stock, cash, creditors, goods purchased for sale
Current liabilities	Current 'short-term' debts	Debtors, bank loans
Tangible assets	'Physical' capital assets	Property, equipment, furniture
Intangible assets	'Non-physical' capital assets	Brand name, brand equity, patents, trust, goodwill

Budgets

Companies use budgets to help manage project costs and cash flows, to forecast future financial performance. Budget plans establish whether there is a surplus (profit) or a shortfall (loss). Typically, project managers record all costs incurred on a project against the budget allocated, at regular intervals over the life of the project. In the event money is over or under spent, budgets help establish priorities and adaptations as necessary to get project spending back on track. A budget report communicates the current status of a budget against what has been spent to date.

Typically, the 'executive level' of large organisations has a broad idea of where the organisation is heading, primarily in terms of its revenue and its associated level of expenditure. The executive will ascertain from managers, for example at the business unit and project level, their projected level of income and costs.

There are two approaches to budgeting. The first approach is where managers are asked what they expect their costs to be – a 'bottom-up' approach. The second approach is where the executive tell managers the total amount they will be given to allocate across their expected costs. This is known as a 'top-down' approach. In both cases, there are usually many debates and several iterations of the budget proposed before the full working document is agreed.

Project costing

In large organisations, costs are managed at either a cost centre level or a project level. The project level is at a level below the cost centre, and the manager only deals with the costs and revenues incurred at that level. Project level costs are recorded in management accounts and are not part of the financial accounting process. (For example, they will not be itemised in the Annual Reports unless they are very important; more typically, they appear in the income statements and balance sheets of the Financial Reports.)

Typically, executive management is only interested in reviewing reports at a cost centre level. Functional budgets and outgoings, and project budgets and outgoings, are managed with the aid of project management tools and processes. Using project costing, managers can budget and keep track of how much each 'project' or function is costing, and can take into account their own costs as well as other organisational or infrastructure costs.

At the project level, managers will generate their budgets by allocating the costs of, for example, the number of people working on the project, and then input this cost into the budget at the cost centre level. In effect, this gives the manager the evidence needed to support their request for a particular level of budgetary support from the executive. Once budgets are set, they can be used to evaluate performance targets and goals.

Table 10. When managing cash flows, projects/company costs and future financial performance, it is necessary to have different types of budgets running concurrently within an organisation. Three of these budgets are described below. These will be taken into account within the overall 'big picture' company budget.

Table 11. Budgets are planned to ensure that the proposed expenditure as measured against projected income is justifiable from a business point of view, as demonstrated in the table (bottom).

Table 10: Types of budgets

	Purpose	Includes
Cash budget	The achievement of appropriate cash balances – to stay in business	All cash payments (cash flows) in and out of the organisation
Operating budget	The achievement of profits – to help grow the organisation	Revenues, variable and fixed costs to help grow the organisation
Capital budget (also called asset budget)	The achievement of an appropriate asset base – to invest for long-term success	Capital assets/fixed assets (purchases and sales)

Source: CIMA, 2005

Table 11: Budget planning

Item	Examples	£
Monthly income/turnover	Fees, payments, sponsorship	
Monthly expenditure	Unit cost, cost of sales, production overheads (with cost centres)	
Fixed costs	Resources, salaries, sub-contractors, equipment hire, consumables, journal subscriptions, rent and rates; light and heat; insurance; administration, sales and expenses; finance and legal expenses	
Variable costs	Subsistence, travel, hospitality, stationery, printing, courier services, books, equipment, materials; marketing, advertising and PR	
Miscellaneous		
Total monthly income		
Profit margin	Mark-up	
Fee charged	Fee charged to client for services	
Gross income	Fees + profit margin	

Forecasting

While a budget is prepared *in advance* of the period it covers, a forecast is prepared during the period it *actually* covers. It is informed by what actually happened; that is, the real revenues generated and costs incurred so far during the given period. Forecasts are usually performed monthly, and are compared to the budget to see how the business is performing against this document and the executive's expectations.

Project costing for design

Design is a resource that has to be paid for by the client. Understanding client expectations when setting a price for work is never easy, but there are guidelines for establishing a 'fair' price.

When a design agency is anticipating how much a client project will cost to deliver, they estimate the costs that will be incurred in the delivery of the project in terms of money, time, people, equipment and other resources. They add a profit margin (mark-up) to these costs, and agree or negotiate what the total fee for the project will be.

A budget is then set up, and it is updated at agreed intervals throughout the life of the project as a 'budget status report'. Costing estimates are based on: (1) previous experience, (2) benchmarking against previous projects or industry standards (for example, design industry salary surveys), or (3) advice sought from consultants and other project cost experts.

The budget itself may not be disclosed to the client, but the breakdown of how their fee is spent will be. Typically, clients want to know how much money a project will cost and how their money will be spent. This is usually communicated in a statement of expenses. The client is also likely to want to know what value the project will bring to the client company, since sponsoring or paying for the design project is an investment of the client's capital.

If a design agency can determine the benefit that a project will bring to a company, they may conduct a 'cost benefit analysis' and price their services accordingly. From an accounting point of view, if a project can be considered 'capital' in nature (that is, it has an enduring benefit), then it can be capitalised in the company's books. One of the benefits of this approach is that the costs will be depreciated over a number of years rather than expensed in the current period.

To calculate the hourly billable rate for a single design team member (assuming most of their time is spent working on client projects), divide their salary by 1500 hours. Overall consultancy rates can be used to estimate whether a job can be completed profitably: is the price for the job sufficient to cover the design time and overheads?

Diagram 12. 'Breakeven' is a term used to assess the point at which a profit is made – when there is a return on investment (ROI). The variable costs plus the fixed costs add up to the total costs. At the breakeven point, the total costs equal the sales made, resulting in a profit. A breakeven analysis as shown in Diagram 12 indicates how many units need to be sold before a profit can be made.

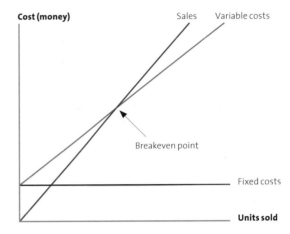

Diagram 12:
**Assessing
breakeven point**

Table 12. When calculating costs to determine pricing structures for product and project costing, it is important not to underestimate the costs likely to be incurred. Table 12 identifies the breakdown of costs incurred in the delivery of the project

Table 12: Calculating costs to determine pricing structures

	Product Costing	**Project Costing**	**Note**
Purpose	Stock valuation; planning and controlling costs; determining selling prices	Planning and controlling costs; determining fee scales	Integrated costing versus piece-based costing
Most relevant costs	Unit cost, production overheads (with cost centres)	Time, people (salaries/charge-out rates), equipment, production overheads (with cost centres)	People can be charged out at an hourly or daily rate, a flat fee or a retainer
Total cost			
Sales price			Cost + mark-up
Gross margin			Gross profit
Contribution			Sales – variable costs
Price			
Profit			

Measuring performance

Performance measures (or metrics) are an internal mechanism that organisations use to drive performance though attaining (or surpassing) defined targets. They are also used to demonstrate the efficient and effective use of budgets.

Performance targets

The goal of measurement performance is to improve the internal and external operations of products and services offered to customers. Performance targets are intended to incentivise success through recognition and reward; however, how a company measures success, and what is defined as being of 'value', can be very influential on organisational behaviour. Typically, 'what gets measured gets done.'

Within a large organisation, each business unit, department or product portfolio will have its own assigned performance targets and measures (also known as KPI or key performance indicators) for which they will be held accountable.

Performance measures and targets link to budgets (to demonstrate efficient and effective use of finances); to the organisational mission and vision (to demonstrate adherence to the purpose of the organisation); and to business and operational strategies (to demonstrate how each business unit is defining business objectives that are in line with the corporate strategy). It is important to bear in mind that pressure to reach targets can drive behaviour that is short term and unethical – as opposed to long term and sustainable (Resnick, 2009).

Evaluating financial performance

When evaluating the financial performance of products and customers, it is important to develop suitable approaches to setting 'good' performance measures and targets that help drive – not undermine – individual and business unit performance, and subsequently the overall corporate strategy. Bad practice, such as manipulating figures to misrepresent the true scenario, can happen – for example, by moving data between time periods so as to create a false impression of achievement (Fisher and Downes, 2009).

Often, this is because the metrics and targets have been externally imposed to fulfil the needs of hierarchical reporting structures, yet the internal team tasked with fulfilling the measures do not gain any benefit, individually or operationally. In addition, organisations tend to measure past performance as an indicator of future performance, instead of setting performance targets that encourage taking action for the future. As Likierman (2007) states: 'measurement needs to provide the context for better decisions to guide where the organisation is going, rather than focusing wholly or mainly on past performance and the current position.'

For design managers, it is especially important to understand – and if necessary, invent – ways that performance can be measured. When design success is aligned with other company success measures, the perception of design as a valuable resource within the organisation will inevitably be improved.

Diagram 13:
The radar chart

strategic
uniqueness
financial
user need
technical
market

Diagram 13. The radar chart is used to plot different variables on an axis, and connect the variables into a 'spider diagram' of data points. In this way, different performance criteria and measures can be compared and evaluated in relation to each other.

The balanced scorecard is a performance management tool for balancing both short- and long-term, and financial and non-financial, measures. First defined by Kaplan and Norton (1996), it considers the four perspectives of: financial, customer, internal processes, and innovation and learning.

Benchmarking is an evaluation method whereby company performance is compared against other industry competitors in similar markets. The idea is to identify points of differentiation for competitive advantage, and decide to meet or exceed 'best practice' performance standards.

Triple bottom line accounting defines values and criteria for measuring and balancing economic sustainability with environmental and social sustainability – 'people, planet, profit'. It is closely linked to CSR.

Examples of qualitative and quantitative performance measures:

Qualitative: Aesthetics, perceived quality, reputation, long-term learning and skills development, durability, ergonomics, safety, value for money, awards, PR/peer reviews, improved brand image, improved product and service quality, improved user experience, better customer service and communication, customer satisfaction, brand awareness.

Quantitative: Profit and loss, revenue, cash flow, cash generation, selling cost, share price, payback period, time, customer retention, brand recognition, process performance, market share/penetration, royalties, patents, reduced costs/savings, reduced waste, reduced overheads.

Measuring value in design

1

Non-financial measures are especially important in how design is valued by an organisation, and how we talk about the value of design. Not everything can be quantified and frequently even accountants have to make assumptions about value and cost.

How can design managers find opportunities, within an organisation's key financial and performance measures, to increase revenue and market share? Where can design add value and be part of the solution to the needs of business, society and the environment?

Return on investment

Return on investment (ROI) identifies how much profit or cost saving is realised by any project, initiative or resource in which an investment is made. Typically, objectives and performance measures are attached to the business case for a particular proposal, so that meeting (or exceeding, or failing to meet) the objectives and measures can demonstrate the 'return on investment'.

ROI is usually measured financially, however there are new initiatives to extend how return on investment is measured – methods that are much more sympathetic to the nature and agendas of design, society and sustainability.

123

1, 2. Since its devastation in World War II, Rotterdam has been a centre of urban regeneration and architectural innovation. The Lloyd Quarter – a former dock area north of the river – is being transformed and is helping to diversify Rotterdam's economy by promoting the audiovisual industries (facing page and above). Mei Architects and Planners converted a former power station into 'Schiecentrale 25kV', which contains studio space for TV and film production and subsidised rental units for creative start-up activities. (*Source: Regarding Rotterdam, 2005 (Mei Architects and Planners/Rotterdam Development Corporation)*)

Example 1: design awards criteria

Recognising the potential for design to engage in economic opportunities, social innovation and cultural enrichment, the Design Management Europe Award (DME) celebrates excellence in design management practices.

The award is based on performance criteria that include: leadership in design innovation (defining and implementing a vision for the whole organisation); driving change through design (identifying significant changes within an organisation where design has played a major role); excellence in design coordination (demonstrating capabilities, processes, skills and resources); and strategic performance (demonstrating performance based on objectives, deliverables and the results – both tangible and intangible) (<www.designmanagementeurope.com>).

Example 2: social return on investment

Social return on investment (SROI) identifies how to quantify and monetise social value creation, for example, non-profit organisations that create social value. REDF has created a SROI Framework that identifes direct, demonstrable cost savings and revenue contributions associated with an individual's employment in a social purpose enterprise.

Example 3: measures of business activity

Measures include: tracking social outcomes, increase in levels of self-esteem and social support systems, or improvements in housing stability. Their approach also investigates the idea of 'investment philanthropy' and the measure of value from the three perspectives of: economic (enterprise value), social (social purpose value) and socio-economic (blended value) (<www.redf.org>).

With regard to sustainability, Andrew Likierman's research into performance reporting outlines why and how organisations should use more forward-looking measures of business activity, to supplement the propensity to report only on past financial performance (Williams, in PARC, 2007).

Williams suggests two key concepts for improving existing organisational performance measures: sustainability (the ability of the organisation to sustain its current business model), and resilience (the organisation's ability to dynamically reinvent its business model as circumstances change), both of which 'aim to look beyond yesterday's measures of success and focus more upon the organisation's ability to adapt to what will make it successful in the future' (PARC, 2007).

This approach is much more in tune with the ability of design methods and processes to uncover and communicate future needs – in people, in society and in business.

124

3. Stroom is part of the Schiecentrale, 'the bouncing heart' of the audio-visual and film industry of Rotterdam. It is a bar, lounge, kitchen and hotel that Stroom has created as a platform for young entrepreneurs in new media businesses. The interiors were transformed by Stars Design, and the high ceilings and immense public spaces opened up opportunities to renew the look and feel of the disused power station in keeping with the Stroom hotel concept.

125

Phelophepa Healthcare Train: delivering value

There are many different ways to consider how businesses deliver 'value'. Phelophepa, the world's first healthcare train, has been providing inexpensive, accessible, essential healthcare services to rural communities in South Africa since 1994. It is a 'miracle' health train offering primary care facilities directly to poor and disadvantaged people living in remote locations, who would otherwise have no access to healthcare. The train brings access to on-board services, and more importantly, to 'edu-care' community outreach educational programmes designed to encourage individuals and communities to look after their own health.

Healthcare service offer

The train aims to provide services, especially for those who are poverty stricken and in dire need of basic healthcare. Each step of the process of service delivery is embedded with the values of integrity, human dignity and sustainable economic growth. Professionals from many different institutions learn from each other and work together in delivering eye care, dental care, x-rays, counselling, medicine and healthcare. In addition, screening for cancer, diabetes, TB and eye testing with provision of spectacles is also offered. There are also edu-care services available: education and screening is Phelophepa's primary objective, in order to make people aware of their own health.

Business and finance

Transnet, a transport and logistics group, funds the train privately as a 'development enterprise'. Having made a commitment to social responsibility as part of their business, the company set up the Transnet Foundation – the social responsibility division of Transnet Group – and established five portfolios whose main responsibility is to implement socio-economic development projects. The CSR portfolios are: education, health, sport, arts and culture and containerised assistance. The 'containerised assistance programme' is Transnet Foundation's creative solution to addressing the shortage of infrastructure and service delivery in rural communities. This programme has been innovative in utilising old or damaged freight containers, which are repaired and custom made to meet the social services and safety and security needs of rural communities.

The train also receives support from philanthropic donors, including Colgate and Roche, and other local, regional and international sponsors. Transnet's capital investment was approximately 15 million rand (US $1.9 million), with a monthly operational budget of an estimated 1.2 million rand (US $150,000) in 2009. For the users of the train's services, fees are minimal, with some services being offered free of charge.

1. The name Phelophepa comes from a combination of Setswana and Sesotho, which literally means good, clean health. The train is 360 metres long and currently services more than 180,000 individuals annually. There are 19 full time staff and 36 final-year medical students who work with and learn from each other on the train as they use the latest technology to treat over 1000 people a week.

1

According to Transnet: 'the business agenda of our social responsibility programmes is developmental, but the business processes are aligned to that of Transnet, a company that prides itself in complying with good corporate governance practices.' Transnet screen every potential and current programme in terms of sustainability and the impact they make – as a social and financial investment, but also with a view to enhancing opportunities for the growth of both the company and the wider South African economy.

2, 3. Upon arrival, there is a main registration 'waiting area' where patients register to use the services offered (top). After registration, patients are channelled to the appropriate clinic according to the need of the patient, whether it be dental, health or eye clinic (above).

Design and marketing

Phelophepa's ingenious design ensures that there is electricity during its five stationary days: a power supply is vital for the provision of the dental and medical services offered.

What began as a three-coach initiative now extends to 16 fully equipped compartments with clinics, cubicles and other communication facilities.

Staff and students have access to card phones, telephones, fax machines, the Internet and a kitchen with the capacity to prepare 220 meals per day.

Local newspapers and radio stations assist with marketing the train by placing adverts at nominal prices. The marketing managers of Phelophepa elect people from rural areas to build relationships between patients and those aboard. Teams travel annually from January – September following a scheduled route. A week is spent in each area. The train will only return to a previously visited vicinity after two years.

4. The staff – nurses, dentists, optometrists, pharmacists, edu-clinic specialists, psychologists and final year medical students – have treated over half a million patients during the past 14 years.

4

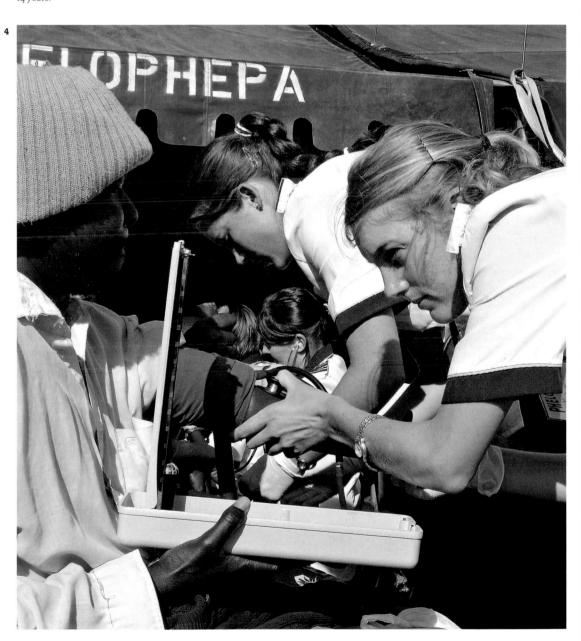

Thomas Lockwood
Design Management Institute

Dr Lockwood is responsible for all aspects of managing the Institute in order to support the international design management community by helping organisations worldwide better understand the effective management of design for economic growth. This includes setting the research agenda, operations management, and managing member programmes throughout the world.

Measuring value in design: the imperative for integrated design management

'The role of design in business has shifted dramatically over the past few years. Design is now recognised as a key business process as well as an asset that can add significant value. Yet few business professionals – or design professionals, for that matter – know how to manage design or how to integrate design principles and design thinking into the organisation. Becoming a more design-minded organisation requires synthesis – the combining of two or more elements to create something new.

'Design is now recognised by business as being a process as much as it is an artifact, communication or environment. What many now call "Design 3.0" is integral to business success. It's not what design *is* that matters, it's what design *does*. And the role of the designer has shifted from solving simple problems to solving complex problems, and from working independently in a single-discipline focus to working collaboratively with cross-functional teams. In addition, design is not only integral to the process of developing new processes, products and services, and to enabling innovation; but it can also add significant value to the "triple bottom line". The social, economic, and environmental – or people, profit, and planet – areas are more crucial than ever. The value of design is incredibly powerful, versatile, and far-reaching, as is the role of the design manager, too.

'In my position as president at DMI, I have a "macro" view of the international design and design leadership community, and a "micro" view of the individual players and their processes. There are several over-arching concepts and methods required for developing a more design-minded organisation and for empowering innovation.

'The key is to create a clear strategy and plan of action to integrate design and design thinking principles into business, and to define and empower design management and leadership to do so. Becoming a design-minded organisation is challenging and takes time, but with the right planning, and a little nurturing and patience, it is not as difficult as it might first appear.

'First, becoming a design-minded organisation is not about proprietary processes and techniques; it's about empowerment and transparency of ideas and methods, and being open-minded to change. The real value of design is in discovering and solving all manner of problems, not just fine-tuning physical outputs.

'Design can be viewed as a way of knowing through thinking and doing – from giving form to ideas to a way of doing things. I appreciate the simple definition of strategic design by Marco Steinberg: "regular design is giving sense to objects; strategic design is giving sense to decisions," he claims.[1] This explains what organisations can achieve when they embed design into their culture, by using design as an output, but also as a means of decision-making. This is the added value of design in business; design solves problems, and businesses have many problems. The trick is to determine which problems are the right ones to solve, and then focus on the task of designing the right solutions.

Thomas Lockwood
President, Design
Management Institute
(DMI), USA

'What is the difference between *design thinking* and *design management*? Design thinking is primarily an innovation process – part of the fuzzy front end, and a great method with which to discover unmet needs and to create new product and service offerings. Design management is typically more focused on the ongoing management and leadership of design processes, operations, projects, and outputs (that is, products, services, communications, environments and interactions). Design leadership and design strategy can be viewed as outputs of effective design thinking and design management. Design strategy sets the direction and the roadmap; and design leadership lies in the areas of integrating design into business for continuous improvement, as well as obtaining a competitive advantage for the business.

'Today's design manager must integrate and collaborate laterally and cross-functionally in order to help discover the key problems, and create solutions for both the customers and the business. A great definition of good design is: good design solves the right problems.'

1. From Steinberg's comments at the 2009 Design Management Institute conference in Milan, Italy.

Krzyzstof Bielski
Institute of Industrial Design

Krzyzstof Bielski is currently the Design Centre Director at the Institute of Industrial Design in Warsaw, Poland, and the jury chairman for the Good Design competition. He has most recently been involved in a range of design promotion projects, including Gdynia Design Days, as well as curating Yves Béhar's Design for Kids and Added- Value Global Design from Poland exhibitions. Krzyzstof's background is in retail management, having worked for brands such as SANYO, IKEA, AHOLD and Habitat, and he is experienced in introducing new brands to markets and in the sourcing and management of product ranges and private labels.

Measuring value in design education

'People generally tend to over-complicate what is in effect quite simple. Design has suddenly become seen as an instant solution, something ready to plug-in when seeking a 100% result – with business and with customers. While the world develops more and more complicated descriptions of what design can change, either at operational, tactical or strategic levels of business management, in Poland – like in many other new members of global economy – the role of education in design needs to take a multichannel approach.

'In a highly competitive environment where customers are increasingly demanding, and companies are looking for more productive ways of working, there is still need for very basic work – for example, explaining words such as 'design', 'designer' and 'industrial design'. And on the other hand, explaining what role design can play in business, including the potential role that design management can play in fulfilling business objectives.

'With this situation in mind, and where design is connected with luxury and fashion, we are working on explaining possible applications for design. From an education point of view, we want to make it easier to understand concepts, areas and processes related to industrial design, fashion design, packaging design, interface design and information design – with service design and the design of the actual human interaction leading the way in innovative new applications for design. The educational role needs to be directed at both governmental and local city authorities, as well as at a wide spectrum of businesses, whether product- or service-oriented. The current mushrooming of design centres, design schools and design institutions is creating a good platform and atmosphere for the organic work which is being carried out, and which is continuing to grow. And of course, all these activities create a market for future opportunities.

'The Institute of Industrial Design was established in 1950, and after some recent revitalisation, has assumed one of the key roles for education in Poland in the field of design, through a wide range of activities and exhibitions, including postgraduate design management studies, workshops and e-learning for both designers and enterprises, and business-tailored exhibitions and events.

Krzyzstof Bielski
Director,
Institute of
Industrial Design,
Poland

'One of the key initiatives of the Institute is a three-year European Union (EU) financed project, 'Design Your Profit', in which, through educational initiatives, we create a platform for both business and designers. Enterprises learn how to integrate design into their operations on different levels, while designers will gain an understanding of business.

'Another initiative of the Institute, and an opportunity for small and medium enterprises, is the investment in innovative undertakings through the application of current key thinking, particularly in the area of design. Funds are from the EU, and the project is led by the Polish Agency for Enterprise Development. Such activities help Polish companies to increase the level of their competitiveness in general, but also demand active engagement with design management, at least in the first stage of the project. Hopefully, part of those enterprises will set a benchmark for new ways of working in the long term.'

135

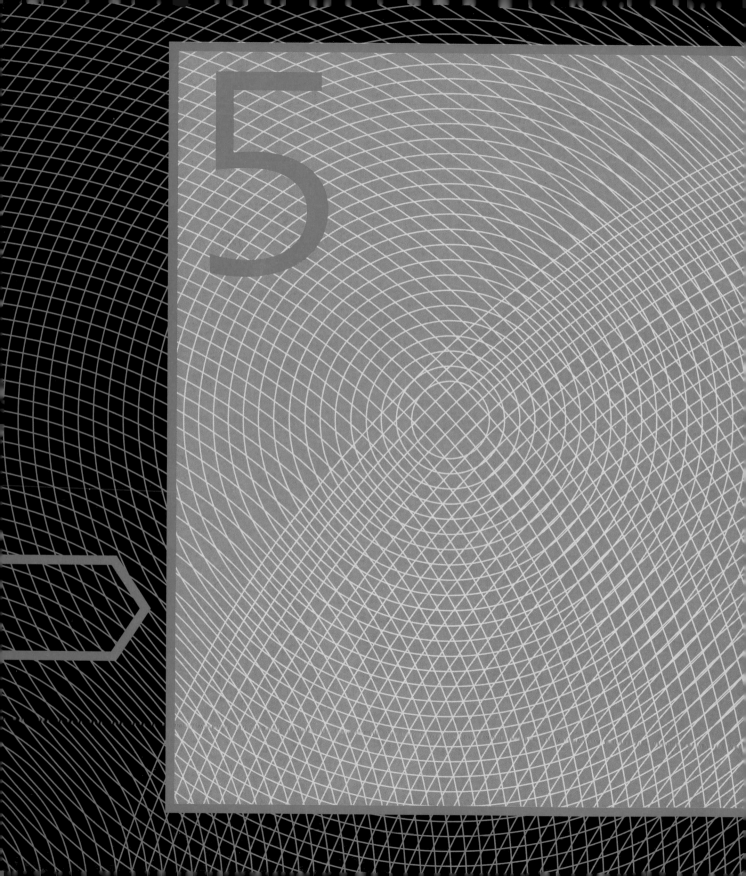

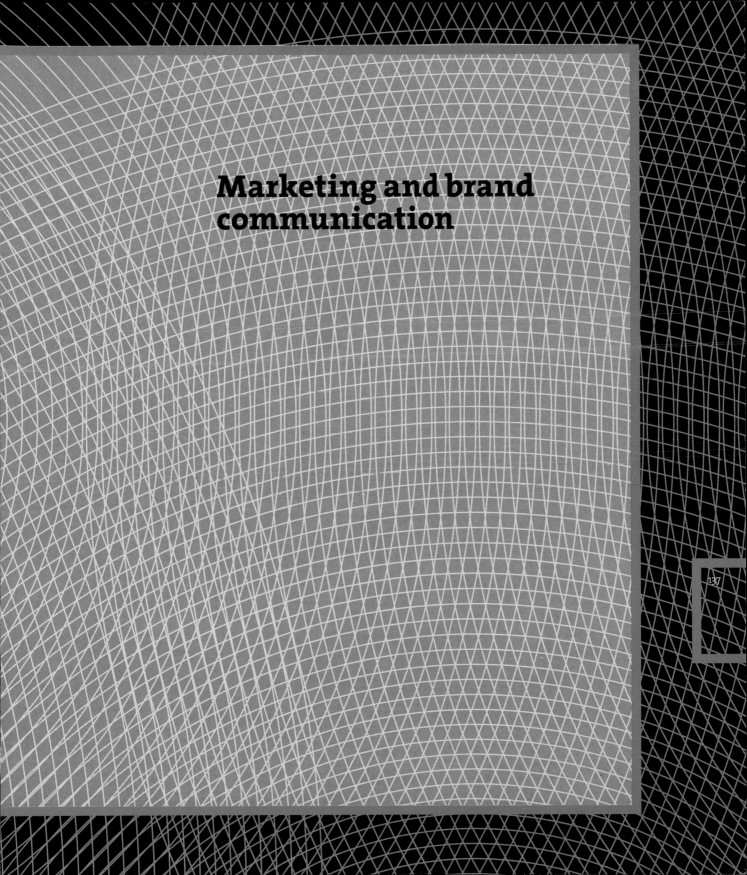

Marketing and brand communication

Users, customers and markets

Understanding users, customers and markets is important for any company that wants to build and manage relationships with people in order to fulfil a need, create a solid customer base and generate revenue – and give the company a reason for its existence.

Consumer behaviour

Consumer behaviour considers the behaviour of people who buy, use or interact with goods and services. Just as people's emotions and beliefs drive their behaviour and choices, so too do people form beliefs about, and emotional connections to, brands that they use and consume in everyday life.

Choices to consume (or not) can be affected by external factors such as price, performance or the environment in which the product or service is located; or internal factors such as what the brand or product image symbolically or emotionally represents to the individual consumer. Predicting consumer consumption behaviour is important, as companies want to ensure their product and service offers are desirable to their target market (appeal), are remembered (memorable), and encourage repeat buying patterns (loyalty).

A commonly used model in consumer behaviour is the hierarchy of effects model, which represents the relationship between consumer attitudes and actions (Beatty and Kahle, 1988).

The model demonstrates how building consumer awareness goes through several stages: unawareness, awareness, knowledge, liking, preference, conviction, purchase, and repeat purchase. According to Pine (1999), consumers buy experiences, not products, and as such, developing a brand image in the mind of the consumer that is aligned to their anticipated behaviour is essential to successful brand/marketing strategies.

Local, global and cultural contexts

Companies, brands and organisations frequently begin by operating in single 'home' markets, and later expand into regional or international contexts in order to expand their customer base, revenue and market share. To successfully develop and grow new global markets, cultural differences need to be carefully considered, as what works in one country may not work in another. Typically, a different approach is taken to introduce a company, brand, product or service into a new market; this can entail, for example, extending or adapting existing brands to fit national, multinational and global marketplaces and cultural conditions; using different distribution channels; and identifying growth areas and niche markets specific to a particular region.

1. Porsche 911 Turbo Cabriolet: in the luxury car market, consumer perception is everything. A survey by the Luxury Institute revealed that the Porsche brand is associated with power, style, excitement, value, elegance, trust and respect. As a company, Porsche has successfully retained its status among luxury brands by nurturing the brand through both management and design decisions, creating product lines and editions that are true to their core values and their loyal enthusiasts (Nielson Business Media Inc., 2009). *Picture © Porsche*

1

Diagram 14: The five stages to the consumer buying process

Degrees of involvement

Degree of difference in brands		Lower cost	Differentiation
	High	Complex buying behaviour	Variety seeking buying behaviour
	Low	Dissonance – reducing buying behaviour	Habitual buying behaviour

Diagram 14. In terms of the consumer buying process itself, Philip Kotler (2007) identified five stages to this process. First, problem/need recognition (stimulated by, for example, a need or want); secondly, information searching (such as researching, asking friends, visiting shops, reading reviews); thirdly, evaluation of alternatives (holding options up for comparison); fourthly, making the purchase decision (influenced by factors such as age, life stage, peer groups); and finally, post-purchase behaviour (for example, keep, use, return, throw away).

Understanding cultural difference enables managers and marketers to be more culturally aware, and so to make better decisions about the best 'fit' between their product or service offer and the specific customs, habits, needs and expectations existing in local market conditions.

Capon (2000) believes that consumer buying behaviour is complex, and that there are additional challenges that marketers face in the international arena, such as: 'differences in language, taste and attitudes of the target market, as well as variations in government control, media availability and local distribution networks... hence it is difficult to determine in advance whether new or different products will be accepted by an international or overseas market.'

Two issues are of particular challenge to global brands. First, the issue of how to translate global brands into locally and culturally relevant products and services. Design plays a key role in reflecting and adapting cultural differences, while at the same time strengthening the brand image in a culturally sensitive way. Secondly, the design manager must consider how to communicate, both verbally and in writing, in a way that is sensitive to cultural, social, political and legal conditions. For example, in most cultures, face-to-face conversations are better for building rapport and trust, and for conducting negotiations.

139

Understanding production and consumption

The web has enabled new ways of producing, consuming and sharing goods, services, ideas and interests, and has led to the creation of new business models and ways to address growing environmental concerns.

The economics of abundance

Traditional economic models are typically based on scarcity and limited resources, supply and demand, and reaching mass markets of target customers through mass communication media. Emerging economic and business models based on variety and abundance, and not scarcity of resources, are now transforming the customer/supplier relationship.

Chris Anderson's concept of 'the Long Tail' is based on the idea of abundance and the notion that endless choice is creating unlimited demand. 'It is the ability of the Internet to reach niche markets that is creating big opportunities.... Now, demand follows supply: the act of vastly increasing choice seemed to unlock demand for that choice.' In addition, with falling distribution costs, niche markets are now viable: 'consumers are finding niche products and niche products are finding consumers' (Anderson, 2006). The net result of giving 'niche interests' a forum is that 'all the niches, when aggregated, can make up a significant market,' and they are 'coming together in a global network, stimulating innovation on an unprecedented scale' (Anderson, 2006).

Mass innovation

People in general and consumers in particular are increasingly involved in building and conversing with brands, as 'co-creators' in the brand experience. 'We-Think' is a phrase coined by Charles Leadbeater which describes how we are moving from a world of mass production to one of mass innovation and mass participation, where collaborative creativity and the shared (distributed) power of the web enables people to work together in a more democratic, productive and creative way. It is also making society more open and egalitarian.

Mass collaboration

There is a growing trend to reinvent the web as 'the world's first global platform for collaboration' (Tapscott and Williams, 2007). They believe that 'companies are beginning to conceive, design, develop and distribute products and services in profoundly new ways'; for example, through user-generated media (such as YouTube), social networking (like Facebook), mass-collaboration models based on peer-production communities innovating together (such as Wikipedia), and global movements (for example, to combat global warming). Leadbeater (2008) predicts that in the future, wellbeing will come to depend less on what we own and consume and more on what we can share with others and create together – a trend driven by current environmental concerns.

1, 2. The Park Hotel, New Delhi, India. Although the design of each hotel is different, there is a recognisable Park style. First, in the bold use of colour – which is in keeping with Indian cultural traditions. Secondly, through the involvement of local artists and craftsmen in developing customised and handmade aspects, as well as through tapping into local economies and local talents and skills. Thirdly, the chain's desire to be at the cutting edge of Indian fashion is obvious, with for example, staff uniforms and bar-lounge music commissioned from Indian designers and musicians.

1

2

Lean thinking

Lean thinking addresses the challenge of 'how to do more with less' while coming closer and closer to 'providing customers with exactly what they want' (Womack and Jones, 2003). It replaces the drive for efficiency (typically eliminating, reducing, re-engineering and cost cutting) with the search for value creation (creating new work, of new value, in new ways). If waste is produced as a by-product, organisations try to find ways to minimise environmental damage (such as effluence or emissions) or convert the waste into 'value', that is, something that customers are willing to pay for.

Lean thinking is based around five key lean principles, as formulated by Womack and Jones, 2003. First, defining *customer value*, in terms of a product, service or organisational capability that meets the needs, wants, demands and expectations of the customer, at the right time, in the right place, for the right cost.

Secondly, defining *the value stream* – a set of specific tasks or steps needed to bring the product or service to market, taking into consideration (1) which steps create the most value, and (2) whether any 'wasteful' steps can be eliminated.

Thirdly, considering flow, in terms of organisational structure, and whether existing tasks and activities grouped into functions or departments can be re-grouped more effectively and productively into value-creating processes and activities.

Fourthly, defining how and where customers can '*pull*' value from the organisation, on demand. And finally, striving for *perfection and excellence*, where all stakeholders (suppliers, manufacturers, distributors and employees) work together to get the product or service to the customer.

3. Porsche has been producing the Cayenne, a five-seater sporty SUV, since 2002. It was a strategic move to extend the Porsche range, and also open up entirely new customer segments in international markets. The introduction of a 'green' version, the Cayenne Diesel, in 2009, symbolised both Porsche's tradition and future – dynamic performance and superior economy (Nielson Business Media Inc., 2009). *Picture © Porsche*

Table 13. This table identifies the shift in thinking about innovation as created primarily in manufacturing, engineering and research labs, to innovation also originating with a range of people, in areas such as financial, social and public services, with clients, markets and consumers. (*Source: Leadbeater, 2006*)

3

Table 13: The ten habits of mass innovation

Invest in creating very widespread capabilities for innovation in public and social sectors as well as commercial.	Innovation needs to be about how products are used as well as how they are invented.
Education systems (curiosity-led) designed for the innovation economy not the industrial economy.	Consumers and markets need to be as much a part of innovation policy as scientists and laboratories.
Low barriers to entry make markets competitive and culture creative.	Innovative societies are good at turning ideas into action.
Innovation is inescapably a public-private undertaking: public platforms often create the basis for a mass of private innovation.	Innovative societies are good at mingling: they encourage people and ideas to find one another and combine creatively.
Mass innovation societies encourage ideas to be challenged and tested.	Innovation has to be central to the story the nation tells itself.

Source: NESTA Provocation 01, November 2006

143

Marketing

Marketing is a process that considers and manages how organisations create customer value: how they identify, anticipate and satisfy customer wants and needs profitably through desirable propositions for goods, services and experiences.

The marketing process

The role of the marketing function in a large organisation is to understand what consumers want or need – a solution to a problem or a response to a market opportunity.

The idea is to create value propositions that are aligned with the organisation's corporate and business strategies, its desired consumer target market, the environmental conditions and its positioning in relation to competing offers.

Marketing experts engage with consumers in many ways in order to develop a business strategy and business plan for how the 'marketing strategy' and 'marketing plan' will help support overall organisational goals and individual business unit objectives (for example, specific targets for product or service lines).

According to Silbiger (1999), the process of developing a marketing strategy falls into seven stages: consumer analysis (segmenting target markets and consumers depending on their needs, desires and behaviours); market analysis (review of the market size, market trends and the competitive environment); competitive analysis (review of the competition, point of differentiation, core competencies and strengths, weaknesses, opportunities and threats); distribution (review of the channels and networks through which to access target markets); development of a marketing mix (an action plan based on 'the four Ps' – product, place, promotion and price); and finally, economics (of pricing, costing, breakeven and profits generated).

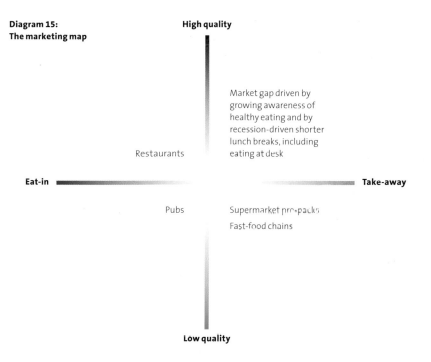

Diagram 15:
The marketing map

High quality

Market gap driven by
growing awareness of
healthy eating and by
recession-driven shorter
lunch breaks, including
eating at desk

Restaurants

Eat-in · Take-away

Pubs

Supermarket pre-packs

Fast-food chains

Low quality

Diagram 15. New market
opportunities: the marketing
map shows the UK lunchtime
eating/drinking market
in the 1980s, identifying
what was at the time
an unsatisfied market gap,
created by the trend for
growing health awareness,
and longer working hours.
(*Source: Bragg and Bragg, 2005*)

Market research

The process of market research starts with the
recognition and definition of a problem, followed
by a process of investigation (such as visiting
places and talking to people), data-collection
(such as conducting surveys) and interpretation
(such as statistical and consumer analysis). The
results are typically interpreted into a presentable
outcome such as a market research report.

Once this evidence is evaluated, a marketing plan
is formulated: one that identifies the gap in the
market; the market segment and target audience
on which to focus; the goals and objectives;
and the plan of action for the offer (product or
service) – where to place it (location), how to
promote it (through PR and advertising campaigns),
and how much to charge for it (pricing).

145

Market segmentation

To help define target audiences, markets are divided into 'segments' – that is, people with similar behaviours, attitudes, beliefs, personalities or needs – which helps to define target audiences and focus marketing efforts as appropriate. It is the role of the marketing expert to then establish how the particular organisation, product and service offer can reach this 'customer profile' target, and consider if the marketing strategy and marketing plan need to be adapted in order to reach each segment.

Markets can also be categorised according to the following factors: geographic (based on location); demographic (which assumes people living in the same neighbourhoods will have similar habits and patterns of behaviour); psychogeographics (motivations behind people's purchasing decisions); lifestyle data (based on factors such as age/stage of life or newspaper reading habits). Mosaic, for example, is a geo-demographic segmentation system that classifies people into 60 'communities' of similar backgrounds, interests and means (<www.experian.com>).

Market positioning

Competitive positioning and product positioning are important parts of how marketing decisions are made, and are especially relevant for design managers. Since design plays a key part in differentiating one product or service offer from another, it is a key source of competitive advantage. Positioning a new product or service will begin with a process of (1) considering the organisation's overall strategy, and (2) conducting an 'audit' of the product and service portfolio with the organisation, and outside in the wider competitive environment. Is there an unsatisfied need or niche in the market? How should the offer be positioned to appeal to selected target markets? What is the customer proposition? If there are many competing offers, is the new offer necessary, in the eyes of the consumer? The audit would also include a review of current customers' attitudes and behaviours, and their relationship to the company and its products and services as a whole.

146

Diagram 16: The Boston Consulting Group Portfolio Matrix

Boston

High	**Problem child:** Products with a small share of a high-growth market, which tend to absorb investment and resources while generating small profits.	**Stars:** Products with a large share of high-growth market, which tend to absorb investment and resources while generating large profits.
Market growth	**Dogs:** Products with a small share of a low-growth, static or declining market, which tend to absorb, not generate, profit.	**Cash cows:** Products with a large share of low-growth market. They provide the main financial return and should be reviewed regularly to ensure ongoing profitability.
Low		

Diagram 16. The Boston Consulting Group Portfolio Matrix ('the Boston Matrix') is used in product-portfolio planning to chart the relationship between market share (relative to the competition) and market growth. It deals with the diverse products or services in the organisation's portfolio, and the different roles that each perform – ensuring that the company balances their mix of products and plans for short-term cash flow as well as for long-term survival.

Diagram 17: The Ansoff Growth Matrix

Ansoff

New	**Market development** Market extension, for example by entering new markets with existing products.	**Diversification** Diversity beyond core markets, core product lines or core activities (high risk).
Markets	**Market penetration** Share or growth increased by, for example, advertising and promotion or reducing prices.	**Product development** Replacing existing products in an existing market with new or adapted products.
Low		
	Existing	New

Products

Diagram 17. The Ansoff Growth Matrix is used to strategically plan alternative ways to develop the business. It charts existing and new products against existing and new markets, and provides better understanding of how an organisation can increase sales revenue through the creation of new markets, products and services.

147

Marketing communications

Marketing communications concerns how the 'marketing mix' – the pricing, placing, positioning and actual development of products and services – is brought alive and promoted to target audiences, in a way that is 'on message' and right for the brand.

The marketing message

Marketing communications (or MarCom) is also referred to as Integrated Marketing communications. It is about how media and messages related to the brand or company can reach target audiences in a way that is most relevant to that target audience. This 'marketing message' needs to be integrated coherently across all the possible channels of communication (for example, used to reach target customers and promote the brand), so that the message is consistent and does not create confusion through inconsistent or 'mixed messages' – which could potentially damage the brand.

Messages can be brought alive through different channels of communication – such as advertising, public relations (PR), direct mail – into an integrated campaign. In the world of advertising, 'above the line' communications refers to the use of mass media such as television, radio and newspaper, while 'below the line' refers to non-media channels such as direct mail, public relations, sales promotions and targeted emails. Other marketing message opportunities include: packaging, sponsorship, exhibitions and trade fairs, merchandising and point-of-sale retail promotions and Internet campaigns. The choice of marketing and distribution channels used to reach customers will influence the price charged and, ultimately, the profits made.

The marketing mix

The marketing mix is 'the particular group of variables offered to the market at a particular point in time' (Cole, 1996). Specifically, it refers to the particular way that decisions are made about the 'the four P's' of product, price, place and promotion. When marketing services, these can be expanded to the seven P's; to include consideration of people, processes and physical aspects of the service offered.

Diagram 18: The product life cycle

Market sales
(sales, volume and profits)

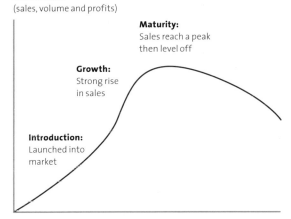

Maturity:
Sales reach a peak
then level off

Growth:
Strong rise
in sales

Introduction:
Launched into
market

Decline: Sales fall,
financial viability
questioned. Seek new
markets for existing
products (e.g. globally)
or consider repackaging
or repositioning
existing product.

Product life cycle

Diagram 18. The product life cycle (PLC) shows the four stages in the life of a product or service. It demonstrates how sales will initially grow as new market segments become aware of it and begin buying, before maturing, and eventually declining. It is used to anticipate market reactions, and to determine, for example, the best time to launch a new product line to succeed an existing one, or repackage/reposition an existing one.

As part of an organisation's marketing strategy, Porter's Five Forces model, represented earlier in Chapter 3 (page 76), is typically used to establish the context of the customers, suppliers, competitors and the market itself, after which decisions can be made about the marketing mix.

Product. How is my product/service similar or different to the competition?

Place: Where will it be sold? How will it be distributed?

Promotion: How will it be promoted? How will it raise awareness, and persuade and remind the target customers of the product? Will I need to employ the services of an advertising or PR agency?

Price: What should it cost? This is influenced by costs, profit margins, demand, the competition, perceived value to the customer, and material and manufacturing processes.

149

Branding

As an organisational tool of corporate communication, brands visibly and experientially connect the internal workings of an organisation (its vision, values and purpose) to the external world of audiences, stakeholders, consumers and users. Branding provides users with the clarity needed to differentiate one organisation, product or service offer from that of competing offers.

What is a brand?

A brand can refer to both an organisation as a whole (for example, Procter & Gamble), or to an organisation's individual products and service lines (for example, the range of washing detergents called Fairy). The brand communicates a 'personality' – what the brand stands for and what it promises to deliver – to audiences such as customers, employees and stakeholders. According to Wally Olins (2008), branding serves four purposes. First, it is a design, marketing, communication and human resources tool. Secondly, it should influence every part of the organisation and every audience of the organisation all the time. Thirdly, it is a co-ordinating resource because it makes the corporation's activities coherent. Finally, it makes the strategy of the organisation visible and palpable for all audiences to see.

Brands can manifest themselves both tangibly and intangibly, in products, services and experiences. Typically, the brand mark (or logo) is a visible 'shorthand' for the brand to help individuals identify, differentiate and choose between competing offers.

One of the most important functions of a brand is to build a positive 'brand image' in the mind of the consumer – a lasting impression that connects that particular brand with positive values such as quality, luxury or integrity – associations that then form a strong connection between the person and the brand.

Historically, brands were a mark of ownership, consistency and a benchmark of quality. Increasingly, the idea of 'emotional branding' – the way in which brands can connect to people's emotional needs and desires – is one of the strongest ways to create a global brand if these emotional needs are 'universal'. Brands operate in 'the emotional territory of people's hearts and minds' (Olins, 2004); and 'it is the emotional aspects of products and their distribution systems that will be the key difference between consumers' ultimate choice and the price that they will pay' (Gobé, 2001).

A good brand builds trust. It helps people to choose between competing offers. Brands that are trusted can build strong brand loyalty, by attracting repeat purchasers, users and followers. Indeed, for some companies such as Apple, strong customer loyalty can result in people becoming advocates for the brand, its products and services. In the end, according to Neumeier (2006), the brand is defined by individuals, not by companies, markets or the so-called general public – each person essentially creates his or her own version of the brand: 'while companies can't control the process, they can influence it by communicating the qualities that make this product different from that product.'

1. Uniform is a creative ideas company – a leading brand, design and digital consultancy, not limited to one discipline or sector. They build brands, create campaigns and deliver results through an integrated approach, with a firm commitment to delivering commercial results through inspired creative work and technical excellence. Uniform's values are to be passionate, effective, inspiring, fun and listeners. They value their team highly, as they value the work they create for their clients. There's a sense of having a 'healthy fascination with doing things better', and R&D is key. Their work environment (below) is charged with inspiration, and a sense of knowing where you stand.

1

Brand creation

Creating a brand begins with identifying a 'position' or 'gap' in the market, and then describing a consumer proposition – one that will fulfil this position in the market (market opportunity). This solution, typically a product, service or business offer, needs a brand identity, one that consumers will identify with this position and proposition (and that will appeal to the target audiences). A brand consultancy or design agency will be tasked with developing the 'core idea' or 'DNA' of the new brand – one that satisfies the desired brand perception.

The first step is to create a brand name, a brand vision and a set of brand values. What is the brand called? Does the brand have a symbol and a name? What does it stand for?

The brand name and logo should be legally registered as trademarks for protection. Brand values communicate the essence of the brand – key words that describe the qualities of the brand. The vision and values will inform all future decision-making processes associated with the brand – both inside and outside the organisation.

The brand's positioning statement reflects the brand's value proposition, that is, where it is positioned in the marketplace. It addresses three issues: who we are and what we do (definition), the benefit to the consumer (deliverables), and how we do it differently (differentiation) (Coomber, 2002).

Brand communications

Brands use design to express themselves tangibly and experientially. 'Brand expression' refers to the act of translating the brand vision, values and promise tangibly, so customers can both physically and emotionally experience the brand.

Brand touchpoints

The ways in which people come into contact with an organisation – through their logo, retail shops, offices, websites and employees – all create an impression in the mind of the customer. It is important that these 'brand touchpoints' are coherently and consistently managed, to ensure 'good' customer experiences. Brand touchpoints that are spread across several different types of channels, media and platforms, increase opportunities to build memorable and lasting impressions with existing and potential customers.

Wally Olins talks about the four ways in which brands can express their core idea – through products, environments, communication and behaviour – so that the brand story makes sense across all channels (Olins, 1995). Delivery touchpoints can include hardware (buildings, retail spaces, mobile devices, carriers and platforms, print material and campaigns, point of sale, events and festivals) and software/media (networks, digital and ambient media, websites, commercial and viral advertising campaigns, online communications and social networks).

Brand management involves managing all the products, brands, brand assets and supplier relationships involved in the presentation of brands, so as to maximise brand value as perceived by the customer. Design plays a critical role in brand management, in bringing the brand 'alive' through sensory brand experiences. Frequently, the principles of how to deliver brand touchpoints are communicated in brand and design guidelines – documents that outline the rules of how (and how not) to implement the manifestations of the brand.

Brand guidelines

To ensure coherent expressions of the brand, 'brand guidelines' set out the visual specifications and formal rules for using the brand in different situations. Responsibility for 'brand guardianship' typically falls to the brand manager of an organisation, although it can also be carried out by an external design or brand consultancy, contracted to monitor the correct implementation of the brand.

Brand guidelines can ensure the consistent application of both the brand and its design language, across a number of customer touchpoints. They include: the use of the brand mark or logo in print or digital media; colour and typeface specifications; rules for co-branding, sponsorship or franchising situations; and merchandising guidelines for branded retail spaces. They are especially useful as briefing documents when working with external agencies and design consultancies.

152

1, 2, 3. Ping Pong were commissioned to create the brand identity for BKOR – the 'Department for Art in Public Space in Rotterdam'. The city was in the middle of a process of city branding, including an attempt to 'clean up' the messy image of public services. Ping Pong were interested in the meaning of 'public space'. They realised that navigation is not about simply following street signs, but is also a question of memorising details and oddities. 'The sign of a snack bar, the sticker-art on the lamp-post, the over-painted tag on the red-bricked wall, the stalled train bridge without tracks,

an endless parade of details and oddities' – all were incorporated into the brand identity created by Ping Pong, they claim. 'If you really open your eyes and actually look around, you'll find art in every inch.' The identity (below and right) can be scaled to any size from a large poster to a postage stamp.

2

3

1

153

Vision, values and brands

A brand is a promise delivered. Viewed as an investment, and not an expense, design can help bring brands alive, and add value to not only the customer experience, but also to the actual brand value and equity itself.

Brand promise

According to Philip Kotler (2005), the 'four P's' (product, place, promotion and price) must be consistently designed: that is, they must be inspired by a clear idea of the distinctive value to be delivered to meet the needs of a distinct group of customers in a better, more compelling way. Although Kotler believes that marketing should be the driver of business strategy, decisions still need to be made in collaboration with other organisational roles and functions, in order to deliver the overall 'value proposition' and 'brand promise' to the customer – in a way that meets or exceeds their expectations. The brand promise is a guarantee of the values and beliefs, and the quality and level of trust that the customer places in the organisation.

Brand value and equity

According to the brand consultancy, Interbrand, having an accurate measure of a brand's value is essential to defining business strategy. Interbrand releases an annual 'Best Global Brands' list, and their method for valuing brands is to treat brands as assets – on the basis of how much they are likely to earn in the future.

Their proprietary calculation method has three core components: (1) Financial Analysis (forecasted current and future revenue specifically attributable to the brand). This gives a figure for Economic Earnings. (2) Role of Brand Analysis (a measure of how the brand influences customer demand at the point of purchase). This provides a figure for Branded Earnings. (3) Brand Strength Score (a benchmark of the brand's ability to secure ongoing customer demand loyalty, repurchase, retention.

Brand equity refers to the additional value and positive associations that a brand name or symbol has added to a product, as compared to competitive or non-branded products, in the mind of the consumer. It is possible to transfer brand equity to other product or service lines (brand extension), as the positive association in the mind of the consumer makes it more likely to succeed (brand recognition). Brand equity that is stretched too far (for example, into entirely new product lines) can create confusion in how consumers perceive the brand. It is therefore important to evaluate 'brand stretch' carefully.

1. Brand Union were asked by SABMiller to redesign the packaging for Club Colombia (before, below left and after, below right), in order to capture more market share. A segmentation study revealed an emerging new set of consumer types – the 'worth more' beer segment for which Club Colombia could be positioned as being 'elegant and sophisticated', and competing with whisky and wine, as well as imported beers.

2. The equity already established in the use of the 'tunjo' – the gold symbol recognised in Colombia as representing tradition, provenance and culture, helped to evoke Colombian pride, excellence and discernment. The solution repositioned Club Colombia as the first truly premium beer brand in Colombia, and tapped into the much under-exploited female market. After the redesign a new advertising campaign and the implementation of new brand guidelines, sales increased by 65% over the previous year.

1     2

Protecting and sustaining brands

Current economic models are based on the idea of unlimited growth and development; progress is inextricably tied to expansion, having more, and the notion that bigger is better. In today's consumer society, personal identity is largely based on what you own; and encouraging people to affirm their identity through the images associated with particular goods and services – how a brand image resonates with a person's own sense of identity and self – is therefore key. Expensive brands, for example, are exclusive; while they may appeal to many, they are only accessible in reality to a limited number of people with a large disposable income.

Investments made in branding and design need to be looked after, just like any other asset in the organisation. Formally, this can be achieved through, for example, setting up, brand and design guidelines, or appointing a 'brand guardian' to ensure the brand is managed effectively. Legally, the value of brand and any associated design assets can be protected by registering their intellectual property (IP).

Intellectual property can take several forms: Patents protect the technical and functional aspects of products and processes; trademarks protect the origins of products or services; design registration protects the visual appearance or eye appeal of products; and copyright protects the replication of the original 'fixed' work (usually written) of an author or company.

155

Zipcar: the vision driving the world's largest car sharing club

Zipcar is a self-service, on-demand alternative to car ownership; a service that offers urban residents and businesses a solution to the significant parking, congestion and transportation issues that plague urban residents.

Zipcar's mission is to offer a new model for automobile transportation. Their vision is to provide reliable and convenient access to on-demand transportation that complements other means of mobility. The founders were originally inspired on a visit to Berlin in 1999, where, as an alternative to owning a vehicle, cars were available by the hour.

Taking the idea further, Zipcar outfitted their cars with wireless technology, created a hassle-free reservation system, and strategically placed the cars around key cities and neighbourhoods. Launched in 2000, Zipcar made the ability to drive cars by the hour or day available to the masses.

Customer benefits: collaborative consumption

For people who do not use a car regularly, Zipcar is more cost-effective and hassle-free than owning, renting or leasing. Zipcar pays for assigned parking, city congestion charges, maintenance, insurance and petrol. Members can reserve exactly the car they want from the fleet, which ranges from gas/electric hybrids (such as the Toyota Prius and Honda Hybrid), to high-end vehicles (such as the Mini Cooper and BMW).

Members benefit in terms of convenience, accessibility and cost savings. Each membership fee helps, in effect, to 'collaboratively finance' the cars, whilst providing each member with readily available access to the fleet, for a fraction of the cost. Zipcar is changing the way that people think about car ownership: over 40% of members either sell their car or stop a car-purchasing decision.

156

5. MARKETING AND BRAND COMMUNICATION
VISION, VALUES AND BRANDS « | **CASE STUDY: ZIPCAR** | » CONTEXTUAL PERSPECTIVES: ROBERT MALCOLM

1. Zipcar has made car sharing a mainstream amenity in London and over 50 American cities.

1

Robert Malcolm
Design Consultant

Robert Malcolm is an architect and interior designer who worked at Foster + Associates and Conran & Partners before setting up as a design consultant in 2009.

Global design and brand management

'The Park Hotel Group is India's leading chain of boutique hotels. Its owner, Priya Paul, took over the huge task of bringing her existing hotel properties into the 21st century with the renovation of the Park Bangalore in 2000. Since then she has worked closely with her designers to establish a contemporary Indian style, breaking new ground in the fusion of modern and traditional Indian sensibilities. The brand has become synonymous with this youthful approach, which sets it apart from its competitors.

'While at Conran and Partners, I was involved in the projects at Bangalore, New Delhi and Kolkata. There we developed the brand, not only in the design of the hotel environments, but also in the creation of a new graphic identity for the company, and for each individual hotel.

'There is a Park Hotels spirit which is translated, not copied, in each property. Key to this is the vision of Ms Paul, who sends her designers off into new territories, creating challenges, and questioning received wisdom as to what is and what is not suitable in hotel design.

'The narrative for the design of each Park Hotel is always strong and appropriate to its location. Not only does the story focus the client and design team but it also provides the PR hook around which the new hotel is marketed. For example, the Park Delhi was designed around the five elements of Vastu Shastra – (the Hindu version of Feng Shui) – earth, air, fire, water and space.

'Although each hotel is different, there is a recognisable Park style. The first of the common features in the design of a Park Hotel is the bold use of colour. This is in response to the strong sunlight experienced in the subcontinent and is also in keeping with Indian cultural traditions. Neutrals and pale colours, tasteful and apt in the north, look washed out and dull in an Indian context. Secondly, the involvement of local artists and craftsmen in developing artwork, furniture and fittings, often handmade, is key to Park Hotels' design.

'This customised approach includes decorative plasterwork, tiles and mosaic, fabrics, glassware, wood carving, metalwork, painting, sculpture, and even video. Commitment to local economies makes good business sense and enhances the company's green credentials.

'Thirdly, the chain's desire to be at the cutting edge of Indian fashion distinguishes the Park Hotel brand. Top name Indian designers are commissioned to create the staff uniforms and well-known DJs play in the hotel bars and help compile the lounge music for the hotel lobbies.

'Thus, the hotel identity is carried through at every level, ensuring the guest and visitor a sensual submersion in all things Park. At each stage I was consulted, not only on all visual items, but also on elements such as cuisine and music, helping to ensure that the hotel experience was complete.

'Bangalore was followed closely by renovations at New Delhi, Chennai, Mumbai, Kolkata, and Navi. A totally new hotel that is currently on site in Hyderabad – an iconic building designed by SOM – will be the jewel in Park's crown. Each project breaks new ground, and the Park brand accurately reflects the rapid economic and cultural progress that India is making.'

Robert Malcolm
Design Consultant,
UK

'The hotel identity is carried through at every level, ensuring the guest and visitor a sensual submersion in all things Park.'

161

Naoko Iida
Issey Miyake Inc.

contextual perspectives

As a graduate of Design Management working in the fashion industry, Naoko Iida has witnessed first-hand how Design Management principles can be applied to strengthen brand identity and, as a result, enhance sales power.

Vision, values and brands: fashion design management

'The overseas fashion industry cannot live without consumers; it is therefore essential to not only offer the right products in the right quantity, but also in the right places at the right time. Comprehensive market research and effective communication with industry stakeholders are key to achieving this.

'At ISSEY MIYAKE INC. (IMI), I am in charge of overseas business for "me ISSEY MIYAKE", the brand name used for the Asian market. In Europe and the USA, the brand name "CAULIFLOWER" is used because of the trademark registration problem. My work involves liaising between IMI and its overseas subsidiaries and clients, and promoting improved performance through emphasising the balance of design and business across the brand internationally.

'Each country presents different challenges, but the key issue is finding the best solution in each case that will boost sales and strengthen the IMI brand. Market research and communication are of utmost importance in achieving this: market research incorporates factors such as product development and distribution, promotion and pricing, and competitors and consumer trends. Communication has two core elements; to liaise effectively with relevant parties and to successfully articulate the deep messages that the brand wants to convey. Additionally, within my role it is important to sometimes visit each country and investigate shops with one's own eyes in order to grasp the situation, discuss problems and then offer advice on how to develop the business.

'Effective preparation and communication are essential when selling the brand's collection. This happens every six months in Tokyo, New York, Milan, Düsseldorf, Paris and London, and is attended by many professional buyers. I serve the Asian buyers and give collection presentations for three subsidiaries in New York, Paris and London. To do this, it is necessary to understand both the Japanese and overseas markets, as well as having full knowledge of the new collection.

162

'Before the selling, I work on making collection documents, scheduling the selling and samples shipping, making appointments with our clients, approaching new markets, and pricing the collection merchandise. To do this, I have meetings with related parties such as the merchandiser, the promotion team, design team, brand manager, clients and subsidiaries, which highlights the importance of inter-disciplinary communication within our team. After the selling is over, I organise all international orders and prepare for the exportation. Further, I always ask subsidiary and clients to send me their feedback report on the collection, which I then share with the IMI team to improve future business.

'In terms of store appearance, it is very important for the designer's fashion business to make a store that attracts people in an instant. I send a visual plan guide every month to clients, which is consistent with that used in Japan to create a unified brand identity. Individual stores follow the guide for at least four days from the monthly launch, after which they make their own shop floor; which has to be based on IMI brand's layout principle, according to their stock situation or sales plan. The unified brand feeling appears by having IMI's common layout, but aspects such as individual sales promotions, staff uniforms and how customers are served also contribute to the atmosphere and appearance of each shop.

Naoko Iida
Issey Miyake Inc.,
Overseas Operations
Department

'I try to always advance communications between IMI and the other parties carefully. The important thing is to research and understand when, where and how consumers want to purchase, and then provide the best environment to meet their needs and therefore grow sales and market share. The balance of design (the brand's power of creation) and business (the understanding of the consumer market) is particularly important. Effective communication helps to develop an understanding of the situation at hand, and builds good relationships with clients, subsidiaries and stakeholders connected to the brand.'

Design and innovation

Design, management and innovation

The connection between design, management and innovation is evolving within rapidly changing contexts. Historically seen as a bridge between the internal design resource and other organisational functions, such as marketing, management and strategy, design is increasingly playing a catalytic role by working cross-functionally and establishing the common ground between departmental agendas and objectives.

Design and business

Design takes a user-centred (or customer-focused) point of view in the development of new processes, products and services (as opposed to focusing on internal hierarchies or traditional core capacities); design also envisions people-centred solutions in both the product-service context and organisational context. Managing how design connects with business objectives, strategically and operationally, is one of the key roles of the design manager.

The Cox Review set out a useful framework for the relationship between creativity, design and innovation. 'Creativity is the generation of new ideas – either a new way of looking at existing problems or the discovery of new opportunities. Innovation is the exploitation of new ideas. Design is what links creativity and innovation – it shapes the ideas so they become practical and attractive propositions for users and customers' (Cox, 2005).

Design creates value and helps to stimulate innovation and growth: Scherfig (2007) asserts that: 'good design is created when a company is able to realise the functional, social, and economic potentials inherent in the use of design. It is particularly important for companies that are not able to compete on production costs to become aware of the huge potential of working strategically with design.'

Innovation

There are three types of innovation (HBS, 2003 and 2009): incremental innovation, which exploits existing forms or technologies (for example, through small changes, improvements and reconfigurations based on established knowledge and existing organisational capabilities). Secondly, modular innovation (within one or more component of a system) which, although significant, is not radically transformative. And finally, radical innovation, which departs from existing knowledge, capabilities or technologies to create something new in the world, perhaps triggered by new opportunities or capabilities that become obsolete (radical innovation can also be referred to as breakthrough, discontinuous or transformational innovation). The Internet is opening up new capabilities for design, management and innovation; such as the ability to disrupt existing processes through technology (disruptive innovation), new organisational models (social innovation), and new environmentally aware challenges (eco-innovation).

1

1: Tata Motors describes the environmentally friendly Nano as a breakthrough or radical innovation. The real significance of the Nano goes beyond the car itself: Tata Motors asked people to 'imagine a car within reach of all' – it is the least expensive car in the world, achieved through challenging every step of the design and production process, so that 'engineers worked to do more with less'. Pictured (left) is Tata Motor's People's Car, the standard version Nano.

2

2. According to *Business Week* magazine, innovation is often measured in terms of patents – Tata Motors filed 34 patents for the Nano. But some of the most valuable innovations take existing, patented components and remix them in ways that more effectively serve the needs of large numbers of customers. Its modular design means that the Nano is constructed of components that can be built and shipped separately to be assembled in a variety of locations – they are kits that are distributed, assembled and serviced by local entrepreneurs – dispersing wealth through 'open distribution' networks (*Business Week*, 2008). Pictured (left) is the luxury version of the Nano.

Design-driven innovation

Design-driven innovation involves managing the relationship between design and innovation, where innovation is driven by the needs of users and customers. It entails taking more of a 'bottom-up' (user-centred) approach to adding value to a customer experience.

People-centred design processes

Involving end-users in the design process is a great way of generating new products and services, and can lead to the adaptation of an existing brand or creation of a new brand or market. The needs of people become the driver behind the design of new products and services. These 'real' human needs (not market needs) can inform practical new design ideas, ones that can often be more innovative, ethical and sustainable. This is common in contexts such as public service design, design in developing countries, community, social or global design challenges, and hi-tech start-ups, for example.

Co-design and co-creation

With a focus on so-called 'customer-created value', many organisations are redesigning systems to co-create value with customers and connect all parts of a firm to this process. They are 'connecting strategy to execution, and building organisational capabilities that allow companies to achieve and sustain continuous change and innovation' (Prahalad and Krishnan, 2008). By tapping into a global network of resources to co-create unique experiences with customers, one person at a time, the customer becomes key to creating value and future growth.

1, 2, 3. Developing countries and the clean water challenge: IDEO and the Acumen Fund began a conversation about how they could make a difference using design thinking – and each other – as resources. The 'Ripple Effect' is a project aimed at increasing access to safe drinking water, stimulating innovation among local water providers, and building capacity for future development. Currently, 1.2 billion people worldwide are drinking unsafe water, and despite efforts to provide clean and treated water, supplies often become contaminated through improper transport and storage. IDEO's work started with research in India (facing page, top left) to understand first-hand the needs of the stakeholders in the water system – providers of safe drinking water, people who buy safe drinking water, and people who choose not to. Local solutions included, first, a distribution system that brings safe water to remote desert villages, reducing the time and effort spent carrying water (facing page, top right); and secondly, the prototype of a cart and of a micro-enterprise business, where women deliver safe drinking water in the slums of Bangalore (facing page, bottom). Design scenarios that address water usage can help establish real change, and create entrepreneurial opportunities for local business leaders in the developing world. It is anticipated that discovering these potential business models will create opportunities for solving other critical resource and health issues in the future. (*Source: <www.ideo.com>*)

Brand-driven innovation

Brands that have built up brand equity, brand value and loyal followers who 'believe' in the brand, have the opportunity to capitalise on these assets by using innovative thinking (how to exploit new ideas) to find additional ways to build brand value – with new products and services aimed at existing or new customers, for example. Equally, innovative new technologies and materials can lead to the creation of a whole new brand, one that secures market leader position by the very uniqueness of the offer.

Brand-driven innovation takes more of a 'top-down' (brand and marketing) approach to adding value to a brand through introducing innovative new products, services and approaches. If a brand is a promise from the organisation to the end-user, then the brand vision, values and 'story' become the central driver for new innovations that keep the customer relationship 'alive'.

Design then becomes a way of enabling people to experience the brand in a tangible way through the design of a series of brand touchpoints, which can be adapted to suit the needs of different cultural and geographical contexts. This approach is common in the product and service offers of large corporations, and as a creative service delivered by advertising and brand consultancies.

'Design is a strategic vehicle in understanding and translating the context in which a brand and its proposition are experienced. It is instrumental in distilling the essence of the brand, and then harnessing its power across a kaleidoscope of cultures, interactions and touchpoints to increase sales and improve brand perception.'
Philips Design, 'Seeds for Growth', 2008

1

172

6. DESIGN AND INNOVATION
DESIGN-DRIVEN INNOVATION « | **BRAND-DRIVEN INNOVATION** | » DESIGN MANAGEMENT FOR CORPORATIONS

1, 2. Market needs can often lead to the creation of new brands, ones that owe their existence to innovation, and which use that innovation as their unique selling point (USP). The 60BAG brand and products (facing page and below) were primarily addressed to retailers who were looking to exchange their plastic merchandise bags for a truly ecological alternative.

The 60BAG is a biodegradable carrier bag made out of flax-viscose non-woven fabric. It is a Polish-made, scientifically developed and patented material – and 60BAG have the exclusive rights to commercialise and distribute the invention. The flax-viscose fabric is produced with flax fibre industrial waste, which means it doesn't exploit any natural resources and minimises the production energy use.

The bags naturally decompose about 60 days after being discarded, and so don't require expensive recycling processes. They are the breakthrough replacement for polypropylene-made 'green bags' and to the thick plastic bags given away by most clothing retailers.

Design management for corporations

Championing the role of design and overcoming political and organisational barriers ('silos') inherent in large organisations is a key part of the job of a design manager. He or she has to identify ways to add and create value within the framework of both product-service systems and organisations themselves.

Design leadership and strategy development

Building on the existing organisational strengths (for example, within core competencies, capacities and capabilities) is a good place to start when attempting to secure commitment and buy-in for design, from internal and external stakeholders (for example, employees, consultancies, distributors and customers). For design managers aspiring to succeed in leadership and innovation, it will be critical to position design as a tool to help evolve the organisational strategy, successfully exploit organisational strengths, and extend how design is perceived and understood as an agent for change.

According to Paul Geraghty, design is increasingly seen as a competency that can drive and co-ordinate innovation. 'Each company has a set of resources and capabilities from which it seeks to create economic value. Design can link resources and capabilities to create sustainable competitive advantage... through new product and service developments and creative communications' (Geraghty, 2008).

Managing product and service development processes

Corporations are best known to customers through their external brand touchpoints – such as products, services and environments. Service design is a specialist design discipline that helps to conceive, design, develop and deliver great services and product/service systems – that is, the context beyond the products themselves. According to Engine (a service design consultancy), service design can improve factors such as ease of use, satisfaction, loyalty and efficiency, across areas such as environments, communications, products, and the people who deliver the service.

Inside large corporations, the design vision and holistic co-ordination of all customer touchpoints (in terms of the look and feel of products, services, systems and brand experience) is frequently handled by design managers – both for the internal design function and when working with external design consultancy services. There is a need to balance externally facing considerations (such as understanding the competitive environment and consumer needs) against internal considerations (such as business objectives, project management and cost criteria).

One example of a large organisation with a design function is Procter & Gamble; designers in its Design Function come from a variety of disciplines including graphic design, industrial design, interior design, fashion design, architecture, brand strategy and trend analysis.

The Design Function 'leads the work of infusing Design Thinking into the DNA of Procter & Gamble in order to build irresistible brands that create an emotional connection and delight consumers'. By taking a collaborative approach that works within multi-functional teams, Procter & Gamble believe that: 'Design brings a unique set of capabilities, and a way of thinking, that complements other organisational strengths – helping to bring emotion and the consumer experience to the innovation process.' Design managers themselves are responsible for 'executing key elements of a brand's holistic visual identity, developing new and innovative products, creating innovative primary and secondary packaging, and developing in-store communications, counters and displays for Procter & Gamble's products worldwide' (<www.pg.com>).

Managing innovation and people

Increasingly, multidisciplinary teams are seen as the best way to unearth creative possibilities in innovation. This is especially true for large organisations, where people are amongst the organisation's more valuable (and costly) assets. Innovation is currently recognised as a pivotal management tool across virtually all industries and segments – it is a tool for transforming the entire culture of organisations – within the business and in every team member (Kelly, 2005). New viewpoints and roles are emerging, ones that accept that 'innovation is all about people… the roles they can play, the hats they can put on, and the personas they can adopt' (Kelly, 2005).

Management innovation

Management innovation – the implementation of new management practices, processes and structures that represent a significant departure from current norms – has dramatically transformed the way that many functions and activities have worked in large organisations.

In the context of looking at how to better manage the innovation practices, processes and structures of modern businesses, Birkshaw and Mol (2006) suggest a way to make sense of the stages involved, as follows:

– Dissatisfaction with the status quo (for example, operational problems, strategic threat or impending crisis) and inspiration from outside (in the form of external change agents, usually from outside the industry, and able to provide radically new points of view).

– Then, invention (for example, a 'eureka' moment or circumstantial events), followed by internal validation (understanding risks, overcoming uncertainty, securing internal acceptance) and external validation (independent approval from an outside party such as a business academic, consulting firm or media organisation).

– And finally, diffusion (how the results get to users and markets).

(Source: Birkshaw and Mol, 2006)

1. The DME Award recognises the strategic use of design in the long-term sustainability of European businesses. Virgin Atlantic Airways Ltd won the DME award for large companies in 2008, for their excellence in design co-ordination. The manifesto describes the non-negotiable aspects of the day-to-day business, such as safety and on-time departure.

The business objectives set yearly goals and specific targets, such as the yearly budget or new markets to target. The divisional plan is, in effect, the business plan, which details all projects and targets. The design mission is to 'inspire change with considered innovation, creating functionally excellent ground and air environments and products.' The brand values – caring, honest, value, fun and innovative – are the essence of the Virgin brand.

Diagram 19, 2, 3. The head of design leads the design team to deliver all objectives in the divisional plan (bottom), ensuring the brand values of the company are integral both in the products and services produced and in the actions of the team on a daily basis, such as in the Virgin Atlantic Clubhouse at Heathrow's Terminal 3 pictured (facing page). *Images: © Virgin Atlantic Airways Ltd.*

1

DME AWARD_ DESIGN MANAGEMENT EUROPE

Diagram 19: The Virgin Atlantic design manifesto

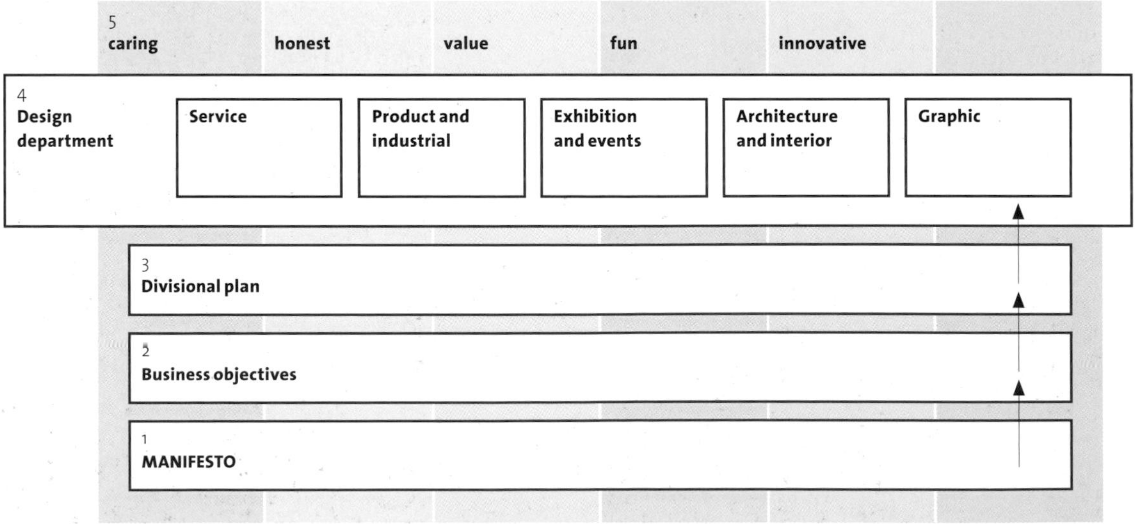

5 caring	honest	value	fun	innovative	
4 **Design department**	**Service**	**Product and industrial**	**Exhibition and events**	**Architecture and interior**	**Graphic**

3 **Divisional plan**

2 **Business objectives**

1 **MANIFESTO**

2

3

Table 14. Innovation is all about people. IDEO have developed a blueprint for ten personalities who have the tools and talent for innovation – roles that are not reliant on organisational structures but are more about 'helping teams express different points of view to create a broader range of innovation solutions', as detailed in Table 14. (*Source: Kelly, 2005*)

Table 14: IDEO's 10 personas

Persona type	Name	Role
Learning Personas	Anthropologist	Builds new learning and insights into the organisation by observing human behaviour and developing a deep understanding of how people interact physically and emotionally with products, services and spaces.
	Experimenter	Prototypes new ideas continuously, learning by a process of enlightened trial and error.
	Cross-pollinator	Explores other industries and cultures, then translates those findings to fit the unique needs of an enterprise.
Organising Personas	Hurdler	Knows the path to innovation is strewn with obstacles and develops a knack for overcoming or outsmarting those roadblocks.
	Collaborator	Helps bring eclectic groups together, and often leads from the middle of the pack to create new combinations and multidisciplinary solutions.
	Director	Not only gathers together a talented cast and crew but also helps to spark their creative talents.
Building Personas	Experience architect	Designs compelling experiences that go beyond mere functionality to connect at a deeper level with customers' latent or expressed needs.
	Set designer	Creates a stage on which innovation team members can do their best work, transforming physical environments into powerful tools to influence behaviour and attitude.
	Care giver	Builds on the metaphor of health care professionals to deliver customer care in a manner that goes beyond mere service.
	Storyteller	Builds both internal morale and external awareness through compelling narratives that communicate a fundamental human value or reinforce a specific cultural trait.

1, 2. Samsung's brand philosophy is to 'devote our human resources and technology to create superior products and services, thereby contributing to a better global society'. They believe in the power of great design, and successfully use innovation, design and 'green thinking' to increase their brand value and market share. In 1995, Samsung set up the Innovation Design Lab of Samsung (IDS) in California, as an in-house school where promising designers could study within the framework of the Art Center College of Design in Pasadena.

Green thinking is evident in how Samsung consider, for example, the production processes and what happens at the end of the product's life cycle. In 2004, Samsung created an eco-design evaluation system to evaluate and improve the environmental quality of their products, for example, resource efficiency, environmental hazardousness, and energy efficiency.

The Samsung Reclaim™ was the first eco-friendly phone offered by Sprint (the wireless service provider known for their leadership in new technologies).

Designed with recyclable components and packaging, the handset is aimed at the environmentally conscious consumer who wants their phone to be 'green' without having to compromise on the latest technology (<www.samsung.com> and <www.samsungusanews.com>).

1

2

179

Design management for small to medium enterprises

Small to medium enterprises and businesses (SMEs) – those with under 50 employees – form a significant part of all economies, whether developed, developing or emerging.

Scale as competitive advantage

Because of the scale of operations involved, smaller firms can take advantage of their inherent flexibility and ability to make decisions at speed. This can be a source of significant competitive advantage when, for example, clients are looking for creative ways to discover cost savings in their processes in which SMEs could be involved (for example, through outsourcing).

Current debates suggest that, rather than being first to market or beating the competition, opportunities for success and growth lie in better servicing customer needs, in other words, 'thriving without winning'.

The four powers of design

Based on research into European design-oriented SMEs, Borja de Mozota (2006) has developed a value model for design based on the concept of the 'four powers of design' (illustrated in **Table 15**, below). Design can thus be integrated into value management models in the context of management science.

Table 15: The four powers of design

Design as differentiator	Design as a source of competitive advantage in the market through brand equity, customer loyalty, price premium or customer orientation.
Design as integrator	Design as a resource that improves new product development processes such as time to market, building consensus in teams using visualisation skills.
	Design as a process that favours modular and platform architecture of product lines, user-oriented innovation models and fuzzy front-end project management.
Design as transformer	Design as a resource for creating new business opportunities; for improving the company's ability to cope with change; or as an expertise to better interpret the company and the marketplace.
Design as good business	Design as a source of increased sales and better margins, more brand value, greater market share, better return on investment (ROI).
	Design as a resource for society at large (inclusive design, sustainable design).

180

6. DESIGN AND INNOVATION
DESIGN MANAGEMENT FOR CORPORATIONS « | **DESIGN MANAGEMENT FOR SMALL TO MEDIUM ENTERPRISES** | » CASE STUDY: PHILIPS DESIGN

Created by the Design Council as part of the UK government's competitiveness strategy, Designing Demand is a programme that helps companies boost performance, speed up growth, increase sales and market share and improve the bottom line by putting design at the centre of business strategy.

Through workshops, hands on support and mentoring from 'design associates', the programme helps businesses discover how to become more innovative, more competitive and more profitable. It does this by giving managers the skills to exploit design by spotting opportunities, briefing designers and running projects that deliver.

The Designing Demand programme is comprised of the following strategies:

1. Generate is a service to help both established businesses and high-growth start-ups get a design project moving.

2. Innovate provides intensive support for technology start-ups, helping them use design to reduce time to market and attract investment.

3. Immerse delivers intensive support for mature businesses with the appetite for strategic change, helping them boost sales and profit through multiple design projects.

1

2

3

4

4. As a small manufacturer of domestic cleaning products, Challs was having trouble getting the attention of supermarket buyers. After going through the Immerse programme outlined above, a design overhaul of branding and strategy had impressive results. Virtually all UK supermarket chains now stock Challs's repackaged and rebranded products; and, after they launched, sales went up by 35 per cent.

Philips Design: design for a sustainable society

Sustainable development is an important part of Philips Design. With a mission and vision based on 'creating value for people', and 'improving people's quality of life', and a design process founded on 'thinking ahead', their people-focused approach can be applied to many challenges across different cultures. Philips Design believe in creating propositions using the power of technology and innovation, ones that have 'minimal environmental impact and are made in a responsible way; all while enhancing people's lives and being profitable to business' (Philips Design website). Thorough research into social and environmental contexts ensures that solutions are fully relevant to specific local lifestyles and customs.

Philanthropy by design

'Philanthropy by design' was born out of a workshop on 'sustainable design vision', the aim of which was to raise awareness and stimulate creative thinking on how to come up with products and services able to support Non-Governmental Organisations (NGOs) in relieving the suffering of people in emergency (natural disaster) situations, or enhancing individual empowerment. Topics discussed were in line with the Philips Design vision, and included developing innovative humanitarian propositions in the areas of healthcare, wellness and education, addressed under the umbrella of social investment, and by rethinking charitable donations beyond financial sponsorship. Two areas were considered: first, internal competencies, technology and know-how, combined with external, complementary expertise; and secondly, people's needs and aspirations manifested in various regions of the world, and more specifically, in their contexts-of-life.

Since 2005, the 'Philanthropy by design' programme has been working on developing humanitarian propositions that address social and environmental issues affecting the more 'fragile' sections of society. The programme leverages both socio-cultural knowledge and Philips Design's creative expertise to donate their extensive talent and skills with the aim of improving the health and environment of the world's developing societies – facing challenges such as malnutrition, pneumonia, sanitation, air pollution, energy consumption and illiteracy.

Specific issues were selected for further investigation using qualitative and quantitative data collection, focus groups, interviews with NGOs and field visits to observe people on location – to gain user-insights into people's experiences and living conditions. 'Knowledge and data collected in the regions were then conveyed to the Philips Design headquarters where they were consolidated into common "digestible", informative and inspirational formats – using "persona design" to represent 19 "day in the life of" stories from individuals and communities – expressing their habits, behaviours, routines, activities and needs'.

Cultural context and challenge

The Chulha stove is one such initiative where Philips' employees 'use their capabilities to face important current social and environmental issues and, in the paradigm of open-innovation, to provide a concrete, context-specific, humanitarian answer to one such issue' (Rocchi and Kusume, 2008).

Looking at the cultural context of potential design and technology solutions is critical to ensuring that solutions are truly sustainable in local communities (Manzini and Jegou, 2003). In rural India, it is traditional for women to spend several hours a day cooking over an indoor 'biomass' stove; however, the conditions in which they exist are extremely hazardous and potentially life threatening – burning biomass fuels causes almost 500,000 deaths every year in India and 1.6 million worldwide, because of air pollution and associated respiratory illnesses.

Philips Design asked the question: 'what can creative design do to help these women continue with their traditional culture, while empowering them to select a way of cooking that does not endanger their lives?' (Rocchi and Kusume, 2008). The solution – the Chulha stove – promotes social empowerment through knowledge sharing, creativity and co-design.

The design process: co-design

Philips used co-design, the process of receiving users' input directly into the design process, to gather insights and feedback from the people who knew most about the challenges of cooking in rural Indian kitchens. These local stakeholders – who had in-depth understanding of the specific contexts and issues – provided an opportunity for 'intensive listening' to the 'voice of potential target communities, families and individuals' (Simanis, Hart, Enk et al, 2005).

Design tools

These stimulus materials formed the basis for a set of Philips Design workshops intended to enable stakeholder teams to think creatively about the challenges. Two design tools/ exercises were particularly useful for increasing the prospects of envisaging environmentally and socially effective product and service ideas – the design-for-sustainability tool, and the chain reaction tool.

1

Research and analysis		Co-design		Co-development	
Contextual study	Appropriate technology	Co-design workshop	Design refinement	Prototyping	Testing and feedback

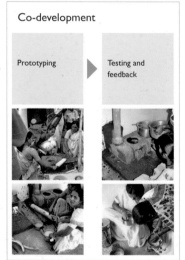

case study

184

6. DESIGN AND INNOVATION
DESIGN MANAGEMENT FOR SMALL TO MEDIUM ENTERPRISES « | **CASE STUDY: PHILIPS DESIGN** | » CONTEXTUAL PERSPECTIVES: MATT BARTHELEMY

1. According to Rocchi and Kusume, 'the value co-creation process undertaken during this journey of understanding and learning has resulted in a stove that makes indoor cooking healthier when compared with traditional indoor open cooking fires.' The research, co-design and co-development process led to a solution that was 'simple to use, easy to maintain, produced and distributed locally, relatively cheap, and suitable for different culinary habits.'

2, 3. Burning biomass fuels causes 1.6 million deaths worldwide every year due to smoke inhalation (left). Philips Design generated a few promising concepts (around indoor air pollution and cooking activities in rural areas), and defined the goals as: easy to access; easy to distribute/install/use/maintain; locally produced, able to reduce indoor pollution; low cost for replication and scalability. Eight months later, the Chulha design solution was developed and tested in the field with families and social entrepreneurs (below left).

185

Table 16. This tool was designed to take into account both environmental and social criteria 'up-stream' in the concept creation phase, and to stimulate a 'systems thinking' approach, one that moves beyond technical product changes towards a more holistic concept of innovation. Its aim was to prompt designers with principles and criteria that could support innovative design strategies to influence more sustainable patterns of production, distribution, marketing and use.

Table 16: 'Design-for-sustainability' tool

Clusters: specific design orientation criteria

Design for longevity: aesthetic and functional up-grading; modularity and scalability; durability; recovery in its various forms; etc.

Design for dematerialisation: miniaturisation; integration and multi-functionality; virtualisation; biodegradability; etc.

Design for efficient and clean energy: solar/wind power; human power; hydrogen power; hybrid systems; etc.

Design for cultural diversity: local resources; technologies appropriate to the context of application; traditional smart practices; individual and community empowerment, etc.

Design for sharing: common use of space, assets, time, knowledge, etc.

Source: Rocchi & Kusume, 2008

Teams worked with the 'chain reaction' tool to deeply and holistically understand and explore people's socio-cultural values and behaviours, before attempting any problem-solving activities. By viewing all user-actions as a 'chain of events', it was possible to identify where their quality of life could be improved through design interventions.

To understand the problem of indoor air pollution in rural India, the teams questioned: first, the causes (for example, the use of wood and inappropriate stoves, the enjoyment of tasting food cooked on wood, the lack of knowledge regarding possible health-related effects; and secondly, the consequences (such as respiratory and eye-related diseases, children's healthcare costs, children's time spent in collecting wood, women's time spent cleaning the kitchen).

The design process helped identify how to deliver direct healthcare benefits as well as indirect healthcare cost savings, more efficient working activities, and positive environmental and socio-economic advantages, at both the individual and community level. The introduction of a 'smart' cooking device, for example, would allow children more time to study (and to spend less time collecting wood); reduce carbon monoxide emissions (and to a certain extent also CO_2 emissions) and wood consumption; and increase healthcare awareness in the family.

The design solution: open source design

The design solution was the Chulha, a stove based on a modular design, which allowed for quick and easy transport, assembly, repair and cleaning – all important factors for rural users. Further, keeping costs low (only five or eight euros per stove) and allowing for cheap repairs, were key factors in the design of the stove (Rocchi and Kusume, 2008).

The design specifications for the Chulha stove were made available for download by selected NGOs (Non Governmental Organisations) as a 'start-up-kit' in order to start the production and dissemination of the Chulha stove. The specifications allow anyone to create a set of moulds and start producing the stove, thereby improving the lives of people in the local area. The solution resulted in a complete training/communication package designed to encourage local entrepreneurial activities in the generation and employment of smokeless stoves.

Open innovation

So far, to facilitate replication, diffusion and scalability of the stoves, design innovations have been recorded in sketches and technical drawings and included in a comprehensive communication and training package, which explains how to produce, distribute, install and maintain the stoves. The intention is to work with the support of local NGOs to allow anyone to use this knowledge for free – in order to improve living conditions for women and children (the end-users), and stimulate local entrepreneurial activities centred on the production and distribution of safe and healthy stoves.

A variety of design, production and distribution models are in existence, which take into account the different needs of rural and semi-urban communities, income level and infrastructural conditions. In the 'decentralised' model, a trained entrepreneur can invest in a mould that is able to cover the demand of 50–60 households spread over 10–15 villages; whereas the ideal 'semi-decentralised' model permits localisation at district level, so that the new entrepreneur will be able to serve 200–250 households across 30–40 villages.

In effect, this 'democratisation' of the value-creation process – achieved by engaging stakeholders in the co-design process – increases the chances of successfully embedding the solution in local communities.

Matt Barthelemy
Smart Design

Smart Design create informed and inspired design for people and memorable brands for clients.

Design-driven innovation

'The need to develop cohesive, integrated user experiences is big and growing. Historically the many parts and pieces of a customer experience were very often handled separately, by distinct groups or even different partner companies. Now, the chances of this non-integrated approach leading to significant innovations and satisfying customer experiences are steadily dropping.

'We have seen this can be a problem for our clients, as their internal structures and cultures can (intentionally or otherwise) enforce a silo approach. A salient example is hardware being conceived and designed separately from software. Today hardware and software need to be integrated, internally on a device and externally through online connections and services. We now see hardware companies developing their own software and networked services; likewise software and service companies are developing their own hardware.

'For design managers, this need for integration requires fluency across design disciplines and team member specialities, and is a growing challenge/opportunity. My own journey started from industrial design and over time, I've become well versed in the many design disciplines that must be coordinated to design and deliver unified and innovative user experiences.

'At Smart, we conceive and design our solutions within multidisciplinary integrated teams. Our design managers work to identify and preserve a consistent vision that is shared throughout the team and expressed across the assorted touch-points. While individual team members will have areas of deep design expertise in different disciplines, there is a shared vision of the unified, branded experience that we're all working to enable. That experience is then designed and delivered through hardware, software, brand communications, online and offline services – all the parts and pieces that work together for a cohesive, branded experience.

188

'In our process, we develop and explore concepts, then iterate and validate our concepts by prototyping early and often. An example of this is what we call "hardware-software sketching", building a series of interactive prototypes to ensure that innovative concepts are viable, and to ensure we can find ways to preserve our ideas intact, solving problems along the way as we work through implementation. This "design doing" gets us past mere design thinking, and allows us to ensure that all aspects of the experience are considered, aligned and well crafted. Our iterations not only keep us honest by proving feasibility, but allow for a thorough process of design and innovation. A lot of great ideas are not implementable; too many that are implementable get defeated by poor execution, or a simple lack of integrating key elements. We can all think of many a nice piece of hardware with a lousy interface.

'We find this iterative and integrated design approach helps us to preserve, communicate and validate our design solutions with our clients, and more importantly with our clients' customers – the people we design these experiences for. At the end of the day, it's not about technology or innovations for their own sake; it's about enabling improved experiences for people that – when done really well – foster positive emotional connections with products, services and brands.'

Matt Barthelemy
Smart Design, USA

'For design managers, this need for integration requires fluency across design disciplines and team member specialities, and is a growing challenge/opportunity.'

189

Sonja Dahl
Design Council

Evidence shows that businesses that increase their design investment are more than twice as likely to see turnover grow. But only a third of companies in the UK have actually increased their design spend in the past three years and 43% don't invest at all. Research also shows a lack of confidence in design and little knowledge of how to go about commissioning, briefing and managing it, or where to turn for help.

Design management for SMEs: a collaborative approach

'This is why the Design Council launched the Designing Demand programme in 2006 as part of its wider aim to support the competitiveness of UK firms. The programme resulted from three years of pilot and demonstration projects testing ways of enhancing smaller companies' design capabilities through a combination of workshops, diagnostic work and executive mentoring.

'The design community recognises the value and impact of using design tools and techniques to help clients get closer to the user and unlock innovation. But what about getting businesses closer to design, so they understand how to use it strategically to realise their vision?

'Through Designing Demand, experienced designers and design managers, known as Design Associates, mentor senior business managers through the process of commissioning design. First they facilitate a structured discussion to understand the wider commercial context and the challenges the business faces before exploring where design can stimulate innovation, create new opportunities and have a positive impact on productivity, performance or profits. They then help the business develop a design brief aligned to its vision and strategic objectives, choose the right designer and manage a project.

'Design Associates simultaneously challenge and support, offering critical design management advice and direction without compromising the business's ambitions.

'Designing Demand has initiated a different approach to design management, one which is collaborative and in some ways educational. One of the central aims of the mentoring programme is to instil understanding and capability for managing design in the business; understanding where it fits and the impact it has strategically. Through working with Design Associates, senior decision makers are exposed to some best practice principles and learn to understand the benefits of design and where it can fit within strategy and goals. It's also an approach that calls for a particular blend of design capability, business credibility and people skills – attributes that form the basis of the recruitment process for new Design Associates.

'The programme is designed for businesses that have the right spirit and ambition for growth and who are also open to investing indesign. Design Associates draw on their own business experience to devise projects, unlock opportunities, build trust and equip managers with design expertise they can carry on using.

'Design Associates don't assume that the business knows or understands how design works. They use a combination of techniques and approaches to make the right conversation happen and then collaborate with suppliers and designers to help ensure the delivery of a project that meets the ambitions of the business.'

Sonja Dahl
Design Associate Manager,
Design Council, UK

'Using knowledge and tools to facilitate a dialogue with key decision makers ensures senior buy-in and the strategic fit of projects.'

Simon May
August

contextual perspectives

August is an innovation catalyst company based in London, UK. August believe that innovation is the platform to sustain growth and that to do this a business needs to focus on six core areas: people, process, culture, leadership, tools and ecosystems.

Design management and innovation

'People innovate; not machines, not computers, not processes but people. Innovation should not just be the responsibility of those who are destined to work in the creative areas of Research and Development, New Product (or Service) Development or Product Marketing. Every member of staff has the potential to influence and add to the innovation capability of the business. This means that all staff will need to understand what the innovation strategy and process is and where they can help. This relies on good communication channels and constant updates as to progress, market shifts and development needs.

Innovation needs a system

'All businesses are capable of generating many more ideas that they actually need or can successfully develop. A system needs to be in place that is linked to the innovation strategy to filter the ideas and select the best or most suitable ideas to take forwards. These ideas need to pass through the filter process to ensure that the appropriate resource and time is spent to deliver on the potential demonstrated at the original decision point. This "upstream" process will ensures that all projects arrive at the development stage with a full understanding as to what they have to do for the business.

Innovation needs nurturing and supporting

'Responsibility for innovation within the business is critical to ensuring success. The Board will need to be totally supportive of the innovation effort going forwards and this means dealing with difficult areas such as risk and failure. The Board will have to demonstrate the desired behaviours so that all staff can see that their own approach will be seen in a positive way. Learning is crucial to the ongoing development of innovation capability and the ability to extract value from every project will enhance the development team's knowledge for the next project.

Innovation requires a different perspective

'Developing a business's ability to look at things differently involves creativity in all its different forms. Staff need to be trained to use different types of tools and to understand what tool is suitable for the type of challenge they face. This might be the difference between a creative group meeting or brainstorm and working with users in more of an ethnographic or participatory way. This different perspective may also challenge the internal view of what the business does and how it does it, so good communication and persuasion skills should be a key part of the creative approach.

Innovation needs to be managed and measured

'Without any sort of measures in place it is difficult to see how the innovation system itself is performing. Most business will look at the return on investment post-launch but this will not give useful feedback as to whether enough or too much was spent to achieve the desired result. Other measures could be used to look at the internal performance of teams or the process itself to ensure that as each project passes through the business, the effectiveness of the system is improved. Ultimately this will lead to better post-launch figures for successful projects whilst reducing the level of unsuccessful projects that fail to deliver or are shut down during development.'

Simon May
August, UK

'All staff will need to understand what the innovation strategy and process is and where they can help. This relies on good communication channels and constant updates as to progress, market shifts and development needs.'

Conclusion

Design management, by the very nature of how it brings together different disciplines, professions and stakeholders, tends to take a holistic view of how to facilitate and deliver the best possible solution for all parties involved. Taking a managed approach to design increases the chances of delivering projects that demonstrate tangible, valuable outcomes, which:

• are satisfying, value-adding and value-creating (in terms of user-experience, or financial or brand value, for example)

• are inclusive and of maximum benefit to all stakeholders involved (from the sponsor to the end-user)

• contribute positively, not impact negatively, on the future (for example, environmental damage or community disengagement).

One of the main benefits of understanding the fundamentals of design management, and the role of design in the development of new business and innovation processes, is a better appreciation of how to talk about the value of design.

This may be in the context of large organisations (where a design manager may play a strategic role and will be able to interact with and rely on a range of specialist teams) or small to medium enterprises (where a design manager may need to be sufficiently expert in all business functions to lead, direct and manage a project on their own).

There are advantages in knowing how to create and exploit value, for example by linking to the vision and values of a brand (brand-driven innovation), or by connecting with user needs (design-driven innovation). The goal, for design managers, is to have the knowledge, experience and skills to be able to manage people, processes and projects successfully, for the maximum benefit of all stakeholders.

Glossary

Above the line – a term used in advertising and marketing to refer to mass media communication channels, such as television, radio and newspapers.

Added value – increased or additional benefit with regard to, for example, real and perceived worth, market value, desirability, merit or use.

Below the line – a term used in advertising and marketing to refer to non-media communication channels, such as direct mail, public relations, sales promotions and Internet campaigns.

BSI – British Standards Institute, the UK's National Standards Body (NSB). It represents UK economic and social interests across all of the European and international standards organisations and through the development of business information solutions for British organisations of all sizes and sectors. BSI works with manufacturing and service industries, businesses, governments and consumers to facilitate the production of British, European and international standards.

Copyright – an exclusive right giving legal protection to the use of a particular design, creative work or other publication, for example, music, literature or art.

Cost-benefit analysis – a process of appraising or assessing a proposal or project for the business case and/or financial case behind it.

Demographics – classifies consumer 'types' according to where they live. Types are assumed to share attitudes, beliefs and purchasing habits.

Differentiation – unique product or service features and benefits, or unique advertising and promotion, to sustain competitive advantage and enable consumers to tell the difference between competing offers.

Innovation – to introduce new measures or ideas, or to make changes and variations that indicate a radical departure from the usual way of doing things.

Intellectual Property Rights (IPR) – gives legal protection to the ownership of new ideas or brand names and gives the owner the right to stop people exploiting their property. IPR includes patents, registered design and design rights, registered trademarks and copyright.

ISO – international Organisation for Standardisation) is the world's largest developer and publisher of International Standards. It is a network of the national standards institutes of 162 countries, one member per country. ISO is a non-governmental organisation that forms a bridge between the public and private sectors; it enables a consensus to be reached on solutions that meet both the requirements of business and the broader needs of society.

Iteration – refers to the non-linear, cyclical process of creative inquiry, development and resolution, used in problem-solving situations, for example, the design process.

Patent – a form of legal protection that grants exclusive rights to make, produce and sell invention or innovation, for a particular length of time. Patents usually protect the functional and technical aspects of products and processes.

Prototype – a physical or virtual model created to test ideas and designs, and to solicit user-feedback, from which a final product or service will then be created.

SWOT analysis – a business tool used to identify the Strengths, Weaknesses, Opportunities and Threats of a particular organisation or market opportunity. Appropriate responses are developed in response to the key factors that influence, or could influence, the particular situation.

Trademark (TM) – a way of identifying goods and services, and of differentiating between competing offers. The trademark is a sign or symbol that allows for instant brand recognition, is unique to each business, and guarantees the origin, quality and consistency of the goods or services.

User-centred Design – a process of designing a product or service experience around the life and behaviour of the consumer or user.

Web 2.0 – a term coined in web design and web development processes to describe how web developers and end-users work together in the development of new software applications and service experiences. It is a collaborative process, involving, for example, web communities, social networking sites and blogs.

Bibliography and resources

Accounting Standards Board (ASB), <www.frrp.org.uk>

Anderson, C. The Long Tail: How Endless Choice is Creating Unlimited Demand. Random House Business Books, 2006

APM, Association for Project Management, www.apm.org.uk

ARUP 'Drivers of Change', ARUP Global Foresight & Innovation, 2008

Beatty, S. & Kahle, L. 'Alternative Hierarchies of the Attitude-Behavior Relationship: The Impact of Brand Commitment and Habit'. Academy of Marketing Science, Journal of the Academy of Marketing Science, Summer, 1988, Vol. 16, No. 2

Birkshaw, J. & Mol, M. Making Sense of Management Innovation. Sloan Management Review, Summer 2006

Borja de Mozota, B. Four Powers of Design: A Value Model in Design Management (<findarticles.com/p/articles/mi_qa4143/>). Design Management Review, Spring 2006

Boyle, D. The Little Money Book. Alastair Sawday's Fragile Earth, 2003

Bragg, A. & Bragg, M. Developing New Business Ideas. Financial Times/ Prentice Hall, 2005

Brinkoff, A. & Ulrich, T. Ten Reasons for Failure. University of Cologne, 2007. Cited in Bloch, B. 'Secrets behind a business marriage made in heaven'. The Daily Telegraph 11.10.07

Brown, T. 'Public Servants – by Design, in Innovation by Design in Public Services'. The Solace Foundation, 2008

Brown, T. 'Design Thinking', Harvard Business Review. June, 2009

Brown, T. 'Strategy By Design', <www.FastCompany.com>, 2007

Bruce, A. & Langdon, K. Strategic Thinking. Dorling Kindersley, 2000

CABE (the Commission for Architecture and the Built Environment), <www.cabe.org.uk>

Capon, C. Understanding Organisational Context. Financial Times/ Prentice Hall, 2000

Chinese Academy of International Trade and Economic Cooperation (CAITEC), <www.caitec.org.cn>

CIMA, Chartered Institute of Management Accountants. www.cimaglobal.com

Clark, D. Integrated Management. Financial Management Magazine (UK), April 2009. Chartered Institute of Management Accountants (CIMA)

Clark, P. Design (A Crash Course). Watson-Guptill Publications, 2000

Cole, G.A. Management: Theory and Practice, Thomson Learning, 1996

Coomber, S. Branding. Capstone, 2001

Covey, S. The Seven Habits of Highly Effective People. Simon & Schuster, 1990

Cox, G. Cox Review of Creativity in Business. Commissioned by the Chancellor of the Exchequer, 2005

Csikszentmihalyi, M. Creativity: Flow and the Psychology of Discovery and Invention. HarperCollins, 1996

Dreyfuss, H. Designing for People. Penguin, 1974

Drucker, P. The Daily Drucker: 366 Days of Insight and Motivation for Getting the Right Things Done. Butterworth-Heinemann, 2004

Dyson, J. Accounting for Non-Accounting Students. Financial Times/ Prentice Hall, 2007

Engine Service Design, www.enginegroup.co.uk

Fisher, C. & Downes, B. 'Performance Measurement and Manipulation'. Financial Management (UK) Magazine, November 1, 2008. Chartered Institute of Management Accountants (CIMA)

Geraghty, P. A Strategic Framework for Entrepreneurial SMEs to Improve Services and Build Design and Innovation Capabilities. DMI Education Conference, 2008

Gobé, M. Emotional Branding: The New Paradigm for Connecting Brands to People. Allworth Press, 2002

Goleman, D. Emotional Intelligence: why it can matter more than IQ. Guildford Press, 1995

Hartley, B. and Palmer, A. The Business Environment. McGraw-Hill Higher Education, 2006

Heilbroner, R. & Thurow, L. Economics Explained. Touchstone, 1998

Holcim (Lanka), Clothing Factory in Sri Lanka/MAS Intimates Thurulie, 2008

Howkins, J. The Creative Economy: How People Make Money from Ideas. Penguin, 2002

Hutton & Holbeche, 'Peter Drucker's Management Approach', HR Magazine, 2007

Ivanovic, A. & Collin, P. Dictionary of Business. A & C Black, 2005

Jenkins, J. 'Creating the Right Environment for Design'. DMI Review, Summer 2008, Vol. 19 No 3

Johnson, G. & Scholes, K. Exploring Corporate Strategy. Financial Times/ Prentice Hall, 2006

Kaplan, R. S. & Norton, D.P. The Balanced Scorecard: Translating Strategy into Action. Harvard Business School Press, 1996

Kawasaki, G. The Art of the Start. Portfolio, 2004

Kay, J. Foundations of Corporate Success: How Business Strategies Add Value. Oxford Paperbacks, 1995

Kelly, T. with Littman, J. The Ten Faces of Innovation. Currency Doubleday, 2005

Kotler, P. Marketing Management, Prentice Hall, 2005

Kotler, P. & Armstrong, G. Principles of Marketing. Prentice Hall, 2007

Leadbeater, C. We-Think: Mass Innovation, Not Mass Production. Profile Books, 2008

Legible London Yellow Book, a Prototype Wayfinding System for London. Transport for London/Mayor of London, 2008

Liker, J. The Toyota Way. McGraw-Hill, 2004

Likierman, A. From Recording the Past to Shaping the Future, Parc Research Report on Resilience: How Companies Prepare for Success in the Future, written by Paul Williams, 2007

Lockwood, T. Design Value: A Framework for Measurement, DMI Review, Fall 2007, Vol. 18, No. 4

Loglisci, K. Interview in London with the author, on November 16, 2008

Managing Creativity and Innovation, Harvard Business Essentials, Harvard Business Press, 2003

McDonagh, W. & Braungart, M. Cradle to Cradle. North Point Press, 2002

Merholz, P. Interview with Zipcar CEO Scott Griffith. <www.adaptivepath.com> 2008

Neumeier, M. The Brand Gap. New Riders, 2006

Nussbaum, B. ZipCar Capitalism: A New Economic Model? <www.businessweek.com/NussbaumOnDesign>, Oct 30, 2008

Olins, W. On Brand. Thames & Hudson, 2003

Olins, W. The Brand Handbook. Thames & Hudson, 2008

Philips Design. Seeds for Growth, Philips Design Solutions, 2008

Pine, B.J. & Gilmore, J.H. The Experience Economy. Harvard Business School Press, 1999

Porter, M. Competitive Advantage: Creating and Sustaining Superior Performance. Free Press, 1995

Porter, M. Competitive Strategy: Techniques for Analysing Industries and Competitors. Macmillan, 1980

Portigal, S. Products and their Ecosystems. www.core77.com/offsite/archive.asp

Prahalad, C.K. & Hamel, G. 'The Core Competence of the Organisation'. Harvard Business Review, 1990

Prahalad, C.K. & Krishnan, M.S. The New Age of Innovation. McGraw-Hill Professional, 2008

Rees, F. Teamworking From Start to Finish. Pfeiffer, 1997

Regarding Rotterdam: Thamesgate Regeneration Civic Trust Study Trip. The Civic Trust, 2005

Resnick, L. Rubies in the Orchard: How to Uncover the Hidden Gems in your Business. Broadway Books, 2009

Rocchi, S. & Kusume, Y. Design for All: A Co-Design Experience in Rural India for Healthy Indoor Cooking. Philips Design, 2008

Scherfig, C. Director, Danish Design Center, In Review of Lockwood, T & Walton. T., Building Design Strategy. Allworth Press & DMI, 2008

Silbiger, S. The 10-Day MBA. Piatkus Ltd, 1999

Tapscott, D. & Williams, A. Wikinomics: How Mass Collaboration Changes Everything. Atlantic Books, 2007

The Value Chain Group, <www.value-chain.org>

Wheeler, A. Designing Brand Identity. Wiley, 2002

Winhall, J. 'Is Design Political?' <www.core77.com>, 2006

Womack, J. & Jones, D. Lean Thinking: Banish Waste and Create Wealth in Your Corporation. Simon & Schuster, 2003

Wright, R. Finance Lecture for MA Design Management, University of the Creative Arts, Surrey, UK, 2007

Young, T. 30 Minutes to Plan a Project. Kogan Page, 1997

Zook, C. Unstoppable: Finding Hidden Assets to Renew the Core and Fuel Profitable Growth. Harvard Business School Press, 2007

Picture credits

Images courtesy of:

Chapter 1

Co-operative Bank: p.15, p.17
Logotypes: © The Co-operative Bank plc.
<www.co-operativebank.co.uk>
<www.goodwithmoney.co.uk>

Royal Society of Arts: p.19
<www.rsa.org.uk>

Alex Ostrowski: p.19
<www.alexostrowski.com>

PARK Advanced Design
Management: p.21
<www.park.bz>

Icebreaker Ltd: p.29, p.33, p.37
<www.icebreaker.com>

Chapter 2

Royal Mail: p.40
<www.royalmail.com>

Design Museum: p.41
Exterior Shot Photographer,
Amelia-Webb; Salt & Pepper
Shakers, Design Museum Shop
<www.designmuseumshop.com>

Bell: p.43
Images: © 2008 Bell
<www.belldesign.co.uk>

Ping Pong Design: p.45
<www.pingpongdesign.nl>

Arup Foresight Team: p.45
<www.arup.com>

Smart Design: p.47
Images: courtesy of Smart Design
<www.smartdesignworldwide.com>

Dyson: p.49
<www.dyson.co.uk>

Moliera 2 Boutique,
Robert Majkut Design Studio: p.51, p.53
<www.design.pl>

iF (International Forum Design): p.55
<www.ifdesign.de>

Legible London: p.57
<www.legiblelondon.info>

Applied Information Group (AIG): p.57
<www.aiglondon.com>

Nova Design: pp.64–65
<www.e-novadesign.com>

Chapter 3

mOma Foods Ltd: p.81
<www.momafoods.co.uk>
Image 1: photo used courtesy
of Akemi Kurosaka:
<www.kattstudios.com>
Images 2-5: design
© David Jenkins

British Council: p.84, p.91, p.93
<www.britishcouncil.org>

Navig8: p.84, p.91, p.93
<www.navig8.co.uk>
British Council Annual Report 2007/8
courtesy of the British Council
(designed by Navig8: <navig8.co.uk>)

MAS: p.95, p.96, p.99
<www.masholdings.com>

Chapter 4

NCHA: p.109, p.113
<www.ncha.org.uk>

Purple Circle: p.109, p.113
<www.purplecircle.co.uk>

Mei Architects: pp.122–123
<www.mei-arch.nl>

Stroom: p.125
<www.stroomrotterdam.nl>

Phelophepa Train: pp.127–129
<www.transnet.co.za/Phelophepa.aspx>

Philip Goad: pp.130–131
Image: © IDEO

Chapter 5

Porsche: p.139, p.143
<www.porsche.com>

Park Hotels: p.141
<www.theparkhotels.com>

Uniform Design: p.151
<www.uniform.net>

Ping Pong Design: p.153
BKOR logotypes/ Ping Pong Cards
used courtesy of Ping Pong Design
<www.pingpongdesign.nl>

Brand Union: p.155
<www.thebrandunion.com>

Zipcar: Studio: pp.157–158
Zipcar, Inc. Print Examples – Creative
Director: Bob Burns; Designer: Katie
Bielawski. Web Examples – Creative
Director: Bob Burns; Designers: iSite
Design, Andrew Lee.
<www.zipcar.com>

Audrey Arbeeny headshot: p.165
© Darian Touhey

Chapter 6

Tata Motors Limited: p.169
<www.tatamotors.com>

IDEO: p.171
Images: © IDEO
<www.ideo.com>

Acumen Fund: p.171
<www.acumenfund.org>

BAG60, Remigiusz Truchanowicz:
pp.172–173
<www.60bag.com>

Design Management Europe Award: p.176
<www.designmanagementeurope.com>

Virgin: pp.176–177
Virgin Atlantic Airways Ltd.
<www.virgin.com>

Samsung: p.179
Images: © Samsung Reclaim™ –
Samsung Telecommunications America
<www.samsung.com>

Designing Demand, Design Council: p.181
<www.designingdemand.org.uk>

Philips Design, Chulha: pp.184–185
<www.design.philips.com>

Simon May headshot: p.193
© Darren Gee

Acknowledgements

Laura Abrar, Ian Allison, Shoma Amin,
Melanie Andrews, Audrey Arbeeny, Liz Armistead,
Chloe Baird-Murray, Mr D Bali, Matt Barthelemy,
Silke Becker, Peter Best, Garrett Biggs, Krzysztof Bielski,
Duncan Bowker, Corine van Buren-Koopmans,
Fanny Cabanne, Lynn Canham, Vanessa Chang,
Wen-Long Chen, Mercedes Coats, Josh Cohen,
Hilary Collins, Dr Lynette Coetzee, Zoe Cook,
Ann Crawley, Sonja Dahl, Pankaj Dheer, Emma Dormer,
Ange Dunselman-Kunzmann, Tim Fendley, Joe Ferry,
Lucy Fulton, Sarah Gardner, Paul Geraghty, Benn Gibbs,
Lacey Glave, Korinna Gramsch, Gemma Hawkins,
Mark Herbert, Drew at Navig8, Alice Huang,
Beth Hurran, Naoko Iida, Thomas D. Isaacson,
Karolina Johnson, David Johnson, Aldo de Jong,
Maarten Jurriaanse, Ian Kennedy, Mara Kockott,
Michel Kolenbrander, Tom Lockwood, Karin Loglisci,
Robert Malcolm, Kevin McCullagh, John McGill,
Lisa Marsala, Simon May, Colette Meacher, Tom Mercer,
Brian Morris, Ruedi Alexander Müller-Beyeler,
Darragh Murphy, Rachel Netherwood, Jessica Nielsen,
Meike Nip, Anne Odling Smee, Katarzyna Okinczyc,
Patricia Olshan, Alex Ostrowski, Miles Park,
Priya Paul, Nick Perry, Biuro Prasowe, Christo Pretorius,
Rakhi Rajani, Vidhura Ralapanawe, Giles Rollestone,
Lujeanne Roos, Phil Rushton, Michael Slack,
Alex Smith, Annemieke Strous, Hazel Symington,
Rupa Thomas, Tania Thompson, Tata Nano Team,
Remigiusz Truchanowicz, Lindi Tshilingalinga,
Tamsin Valentino, Sorena Veerman, Caroline Walmsley,
Brett White, Simona Zahradnicek, Zoe Zeigler.

Lynne Elvins/Naomi Goulder

Working with ethics

The Fundamentals
of Design
Management

Ethical: awareness/reflection/debate

202

The subject of ethics is not new, yet its consideration within the applied visual arts is perhaps not as prevalent as it might be. Our aim here is to help a new generation of students, educators and practitioners find a methodology for structuring their thoughts and reflections in this vital area.

AVA Publishing hopes that these **Working with ethics** pages provide a platform for consideration and a flexible method for incorporating ethical concerns in the work of educators, students and professionals. Our approach consists of four parts:

The **introduction** is intended to be an accessible snapshot of the ethical landscape, both in terms of historical development and current dominant themes.

The **framework** positions ethical consideration into four areas and poses questions about the practical implications that might occur. Marking your response to each of these questions on the scale shown will allow your reactions to be further explored by comparison.

The **case study** sets out a real project and then poses some ethical questions for further consideration. This is a focus point for a debate rather than a critical analysis so there are no predetermined right or wrong answers.

A selection of **further reading** for you to consider areas of particular interest in more detail.

Ethics is a complex subject that interlaces the idea of responsibilities to society with a wide range of considerations relevant to the character and happiness of the individual. It concerns virtues of compassion, loyalty and strength, but also of confidence, imagination, humour and optimism. As introduced in ancient Greek philosophy, the fundamental ethical question is: *what should I do?* How we might pursue a 'good' life not only raises moral concerns about the effects of our actions on others, but also personal concerns about our own integrity.

In modern times the most important and controversial questions in ethics have been the moral ones. With growing populations and improvements in mobility and communications, it is not surprising that considerations about how to structure our lives together on the planet should come to the forefront. For visual artists and communicators, it should be no surprise that these considerations will enter into the creative process.

Some ethical considerations are already enshrined in government laws and regulations or in professional codes of conduct. For example, plagiarism and breaches of confidentiality can be punishable offences. Legislation in various nations makes it unlawful to exclude people with disabilities from accessing information or spaces. The trade of ivory as a material has been banned in many countries. In these cases, a clear line has been drawn under what is unacceptable.

But most ethical matters remain open to debate, among experts and lay-people alike, and in the end we have to make our own choices on the basis of our own guiding principles or values. Is it more ethical to work for a charity than for a commercial company? Is it unethical to create something that others find ugly or offensive?

Specific questions such as these may lead to other questions that are more abstract. For example, is it only effects on humans (and what they care about) that are important, or might effects on the natural world require attention too?

Is promoting ethical consequences justified even when it requires ethical sacrifices along the way? Must there be a single unifying theory of ethics (such as the Utilitarian thesis that the right course of action is always the one that leads to the greatest happiness of the greatest number), or might there always be many different ethical values that pull a person in various directions?

As we enter into ethical debate and engage with these dilemmas on a personal and professional level, we may change our views or change our view of others. The real test though is whether, as we reflect on these matters, we change the way we act as well as the way we think. Socrates, the 'father' of philosophy, proposed that people will naturally do 'good' if they know what is right. But this point might only lead us to yet another question: *how do we know what is right?*

You
What are your ethical beliefs?

Central to everything you do will be your attitude to people and issues around you. For some people, their ethics are an active part of the decisions they make every day as a consumer, a voter or a working professional. Others may think about ethics very little and yet this does not automatically make them unethical. Personal beliefs, lifestyle, politics, nationality, religion, gender, class or education can all influence your ethical viewpoint.

Using the scale, where would you place yourself? What do you take into account to make your decision? Compare results with your friends or colleagues.

Your client
What are your terms?

Working relationships are central to whether ethics can be embedded into a project, and your conduct on a day-to-day basis is a demonstration of your professional ethics. The decision with the biggest impact is whom you choose to work with in the first place. Cigarette companies or arms traders are often-cited examples when talking about where a line might be drawn, but rarely are real situations so extreme. At what point might you turn down a project on ethical grounds and how much does the reality of having to earn a living affect your ability to choose?

Using the scale, where would you place a project? How does this compare to your personal ethical level?

01 02 03 04 05 06 07 08 09 10

01 02 03 04 05 06 07 08 09 10

Your specifications
What are the impacts of your materials?

In relatively recent times, we are learning that many natural materials are in short supply. At the same time, we are increasingly aware that some man-made materials can have harmful, long-term effects on people or the planet. How much do you know about the materials that you use? Do you know where they come from, how far they travel and under what conditions they are obtained? When your creation is no longer needed, will it be easy and safe to recycle? Will it disappear without a trace? Are these considerations your responsibility or are they out of your hands?

Using the scale, mark how ethical your material choices are.

Your creation
What is the purpose of your work?

Between you, your colleagues and an agreed brief, what will your creation achieve? What purpose will it have in society and will it make a positive contribution? Should your work result in more than commercial success or industry awards? Might your creation help save lives, educate, protect or inspire? Form and function are two established aspects of judging a creation, but there is little consensus on the obligations of visual artists and communicators toward society, or the role they might have in solving social or environmental problems. If you want recognition for being the creator, how responsible are you for what you create and where might that responsibility end?

Using the scale, mark how ethical the purpose of your work is.

01 02 03 04 05 06 07 08 09 10

01 02 03 04 05 06 07 08 09 10

206

One aspect of design management that raises an ethical dilemma is that of balancing the need to use design for the commercial benefit of a company or client against the environmental or social impact of the products, services or communication materials that are created. Design decisions taken during the early development of a project will affect a product for its lifetime and therefore it is in these early stages where the biggest improvements can be made. However, design managers may not have the authority to change a design brief based on improving environmental performance or social responsibility, particularly if this will require additional time to research or test, or if further investment in new technologies or materials is needed. Instead the outcomes may be set by financial targets or consumer demand. Is it the role of design managers to make all design work more holistically responsible or to carry out projects to improve business performance only?

The Quaker Oats Company was founded in 1901 through the merger of various oat mills, one of which was the Quaker Mill Company from Ohio. The figure of a man in Quaker garb, used as the company's symbol, had been registered as a trademark at the Patent Office since 1877 and was the first ever US trademark registered for a breakfast cereal.

Henry Seymour, one of the company owners, is said to have chosen the Quaker name and image after reading that Quakers (people belonging to the Religious Society of Friends, a movement started in the seventeenth century) stood for integrity, honesty and purity. Despite having no official links with the Quaker movement, these traits were felt to be an appropriate identity for the company. In the original full-length drawing, the Quaker man held a paper scroll with the word 'pure' written on it.

In 1881, Henry Crowell bought the bankrupt Quaker Mill Company and its brand, and in the following year he launched a national magazine advertising campaign for Quaker Oats. In 1885, the company introduced the idea of selling two pounds of oats in a clean paper box featuring the Quaker man on the front and cooking instructions on the back. This made it possible, for the first time, to buy individually pre-packed quantities rather than purchasing oats from open barrels, which usually meant the oatmeal was contaminated with insects, worms and vermin. Quaker Oats was also the first company to feature a recipe (for oatmeal bread) on its box.

In 1927, Crowell (who became known as 'the cereal tycoon') established the Crowell Trust, which was dedicated to the teaching and active extension of the doctrines of Evangelical Christianity. He is said to have given away over 70 per cent of his considerable wealth and is well respected as a twentieth-century Christian business man in the US.

Some Quakers are said to be uncomfortable about the company's association. The Quaker Oats brand is, debatably, better known than the Religious Society of Friends. This has arguably lead to confusion, with some members of the public assuming that Quakers have a link with the company, or thinking that Quakers still dress as shown on the Quaker Oats logo.

Is it unethical for Quaker Oats to associate with Quaker values without being active members or supporters of the Quaker Society?

Would it be more ethical to strategically combine graphic design, advertising, branding, packaging and marketing to raise awareness of the Quaker Society than to sell Quaker Oats products?

Would you work for this company if you were a Quaker?

Design, in the end, is about creating better things for people. Along the way, it can generate better profits as well.

Bruce Nussbaum (editor)

AIGA
Design Business and Ethics
2007, AIGA

Eaton, Marcia Muelder
Aesthetics and the Good Life
1989, Associated University Press

Ellison, David
Ethics and Aesthetics in European Modernist Literature:
From the Sublime to the Uncanny
2001, Cambridge University Press

Fenner, David E W (Ed)
Ethics and the Arts:
An Anthology
1995, Garland Reference Library of Social Science

Gini, Al and Marcoux, Alexei M
Case Studies in Business Ethics
2005, Prentice Hall

McDonough, William and Braungart, Michael
Cradle to Cradle:
Remaking the Way We Make Things
2002, North Point Press

Papanek, Victor
Design for the Real World:
Making to Measure
1972, Thames & Hudson

United Nations Global Compact
The Ten Principles
www.unglobalcompact.org/AboutTheGC/TheTenPrinciples/index.html